THE

Rule Breakers

PERI B. MANN

The Rule Breakers

©2022, Peri B. Mann

ISBN: 978-1-66783-220-3

ISBN eBook: 978-1-66783-221-0

CONTENTS

AUTHOR'S NOTE

All of the events in this book are real. Names, descriptions, and identifying information have been changed for privacy purposes to protect the innocent—and, yes, most especially the guilty. At times, patients with similar issues have been combined into one interview.

INTRODUCTION

I had a friend read an early draft of this book, she asked:

"Is this a memoir, a clinical text, or a self-help book?"

Good question. I know books are supposed to fit into categories, but the human beings I worked with as a clinical social worker in drug programs, prisons, psychiatric hospitals, and the court system cannot be neatly categorized into a one-tab file.

Many of my patients have been rule breakers, but in order for me to work in volatile, sometimes dangerous places, I had to learn how to think outside the box and also break some rules.

ON THE EDGE

I sat in my small office inside an outpatient methadone clinic in New York City, listening to Michael speak of his past crimes. I'd known him for a few months. This being my fourth job since graduating college, I felt confident I could handle whatever was presented in my sessions with him.

"It was a robbery," he said. Not unusual to hear when working with drug addicts in a treatment program. He described how he came up from behind his female victim and put a knife to her throat.

"You know…like a surprise." This said as if he were bestowing an unexpected birthday gift on his victim.

He continued telling his story; but soon our time was up. He walked toward the door of my office to leave. I stood up and followed to close the door behind him. Suddenly he swirled around to face me. I barely had time to stop before plowing into him.

His six-foot frame loomed over me like a dark cloud waiting to erupt.

From the corner of my eye, I saw a glint of metal, then I heard a *click* as the knife opened. In a totally casual manner, Michael raised the knife toward my throat, letting the sharp edge linger in front of my Adam's apple like a hummingbird hungry for an insect. Michael didn't move, I didn't move.

Over the course of my career counseling murderers, rapists, domestic abusers, and the less violent perpetrators of burglaries, embezzlement, and con games, Michael was my first psychopath: a living, breathing showman of great emotional mimicry, hiding an undercurrent laced with streaks of sadistic violence. But one thing I'd learned on the streets of Brooklyn: never act like a victim, because that was a surefire way to become one. But, I thought, *What do I do now?* I didn't know what Michael wanted, or why he was holding a knife to my throat and threatening me. He'd never been violent when he was alone with me before.

I stared into his eyes—and saw nothing. No clue whatsoever. By this point in my career I was skilled at reading people, but Michael's essence displayed only stillness. I had but a few seconds to make a decision. I grounded myself and returned his stare without flinching. Then, I said:

"Is the test over?"

I guessed that as he continued to hover over me, his need to display dominance over women was in play. He stared into my eyes for maybe two seconds. Then a broad smile of recognition crept slowly across his face, and I knew I was right. He started laughing lightly at first, then in spasms. I stood still until I saw—and heard—the knife being returned to its original place in his pocket. I stepped back.

"Now, get the fuck out of my office," I said with as much aggression as I could muster. He laughed himself out the door. I stood for a full minute on wobbly legs, shaking. Then, I collapsed into my chair.

*

My career as a clinical social worker in New York City, had begun on an all-male unit in a thirty-day detox hospital. From that position I moved on to working as a probation officer; when laid off during New York City's financial crisis, I interned for my clinical license at an all-male psychiatric prison. When the financial crisis ended I returned to the probation department; eventually I became the assistant head of the counseling department in the outpatient methadone clinic where I met Michael.

Despite my education—a master's degree in social work, six years of post-graduate education engaged in clinical work to become a licensed clinical social worker—none of what I learned prepared me for the situations I would actually encounter on my jobs.

I tried to get a "normal" job when I was about to graduate from a college in Manhattan, where I majored in theater with a double minor of sociology and psychology. Not exactly a recipe for landing a lucrative career. I worked at temp jobs all through college: a receptionist, a billing clerk, clipping coupons at a department store, adding numbers in a research department at a financial firm. And what did I learn from all that? I was not cut out to work at a traditional job behind a desk.

So I went to my college advisor and told him I wanted to work in personnel. I wasn't sure exactly what that meant, but I imagined I would be working with people. Later, at a job fair, I met a male recruiter from a health care company who sponsored me for a job interview in personnel management. I showed up to the interview on time, dressed in my one professional outfit: a knee-length skirt, a red blouse (thought I'd make a bold color statement), and low heels. When I walked into the interview room, I was shocked. A long mahogany table filled almost the entire room, and around the table, ten men sat staring at me. I hoped this was an intimidation tactic to see how I performed under pressure. During the interview, the ten men threw various conflict resolution scenarios at me and asked how I would handle them. I answered using my general knowledge of people, and some creativity. At the end of the interview I thanked them for the opportunity, and I felt I would be one of the candidates called for a second interview.

I waited a day for the phone to ring, but when the recruiter called me, he informed me I would not be getting a second look. To learn from my mistakes, I asked why.

"They felt you were too assertive," the recruiter said.

Assertive? What the heck? It was a job that required intervening in conflicts. Was I supposed to stay on the sidelines like a good little girl?

My next recruiter was a woman who worked for a bank. We talked for a long while, and then, she said, "I'll send you for the interview, but you'll be very frustrated working here."

"Why?"

"There's only so far you can go up the ladder. You know what the glass ceiling is? Well, here, regardless of your skills, the men have all of the executive positions, and I'm frustrated."

I didn't bother with the bank interview. Instead I went back to my advisor and unloaded on her.

"Well," she said, "there's a job as a recreational therapist at an inpatient detox hospital for drug addicts."

"What's a recreational therapist?" I asked.

"I have no idea," she answered, "but if you want, I'll set it up."

I was due to graduate in a few weeks. I was desperate for a real job with a steady paycheck. So I told myself, *What the hell, I'll go.*

I arrived for the interview and was directed by a security guard to the office of a woman named Patricia, the head of the recreational therapy department. No one was in the office when I arrived. I waited patiently, looking around at the traditional, if not spare, office, until I heard feet running up the hallway.

A woman, average size, her brown hair flying as if she had just been launched into space, entered the room. It wasn't the hair that shocked me; rather, she was holding her hands in the air and wore disposable medical gloves as if she had just completed a stint performing heart surgery. And to reinforce the image of a surgeon, white gunk was dripping down her arms. Had I been directed to the wrong department?

"I'm so sorry to be late," she said, a warm, welcoming smile on her face. "We're having a picnic for the patients, and I'm serving potato salad. Give me a few more minutes and then we can talk."

As she turned to go back to the festivities, I blurted out, "Can I come... to the picnic?"

"Absolutely," Patricia said. "Let's go."

I followed her into a large, open space filled with people of all stripes and sizes. They were playing table games like knock hockey. A basketball net perched high in the corner, and someone—I took her to be a staff member, because she wasn't in patient garb—sat at a small table, telling fortunes. She sported a schmatta on her head—it was supposed to look like a head wrap that mysterious psychics or fortune tellers wear. I think her tarot cards were actually a gin rummy deck.

But perhaps my greatest surprise was the realization that all of the diverse people I was watching were having a good time together; if not for the patients' outfits, I wouldn't have known the staff from the patients. The interactions were warm, friendly, and most strikingly nonhierarchical. But when the time came to line up the patients to return them to their rooms while the staff brought down the next group, the patients did as they were told. I was informed the detox hospital contained two floors that each housed forty male patients, one floor that housed only female patients, and a psychiatric unit on the top floor.

I was inaugurated with my own disposable gloves, and assigned the tuna fish table.

As I served my salad, I watched the camaraderie emanating from both the patients and the staff. Some of the detoxing addicts had been sent to the hospital, by their lawyers to get "clean" before serving their prison sentence. Others were sent by parole officers, or probation officers. Some were referred to the hospital by family, others voluntarily came in to clean up. Some came just to try to mitigate their drug habit a bit and then sign out "against medical advice" (as their release forms stated) and hit the streets again. The units housed war veterans who had become addicted to illicit drugs overseas and a few Chinese men who spoke no English and smoked pure opium.

By the end of the picnic I had assumed the same heart-surgeon stance Patricia had assumed in her office: gloves in the air, mine dripping with brown gunk from the tuna fish table. After the event was over, Patricia and I returned to her office, shed our gloves, and washed up in her bathroom sink. Then, we sat down to business. Having been on several interviews, I was prepared with my answers.

"So, what did you think of the picnic?" she asked, her eyes dancing with satisfaction at a successful event.

"I loved it. I want to work here."

"You're hired."

*

As I sat recovering from Michael's' knife display—an exhibition of dominance—I breathed in and out several times, calming my rapid heartbeat. Fifteen years into my career, I wondered if I'd actually ever helped anyone. I met with patients only for short periods of time, while they were in the midst of crisis; then they left, and I had no way of knowing whether our work together had any impact.

In fact, my entire career, I'd been surrounded by trauma, violence—and even death: one of my patients was murdered. My jobs required always being on high alert, never knowing what was just around the corner. And now I was exhausted. Not just from my work, but from my own life as well. Was it time to switch careers?

Was my job path just a fluke, or had the skills and insights I learned growing up on the streets of Brooklyn and overcoming my own childhood traumas led me down this path?

I sat back at my desk, thinking of my time of innocence and joy growing up in Brooklyn, even though it had been short-lived. I longed to feel just a little of that untainted existence again. Would a new job in a different field help me find that peace, or did the traumas of human life make such a wish impossible?

BACK TO THE
STREETS OF BROOKLYN

All I knew before getting my job at the detox hospital were the skills I had learned growing up on the streets of Brooklyn. Most of the neighborhood residents were second-generation immigrants; a magnificent population of diversity, language, and cultures. The one thing we all had in common: no money, no government help, like Medicaid, or food stamps. Everyone struggled, and everyone tried to help neighbors when possible.

My mother, my father, my older sister Sarah, and I shared a small one-bedroom apartment. My parents slept on a living room pull out couch, Sarah and I shared a double bed.

I hardly saw my father, all he did was work at as many jobs as he could. Eventually, we moved to the second floor of a three-family home where my parents finally had the privacy of their own bedroom. Best of all, the building had a front stoop—that space where neighbors met, gossip was exchanged, and us kids played stoop ball into the night until windows opened and mothers yelled, "Time for dinner!" To which there was invariably no response.

"Let's go!" the calls continued. "Your food is getting cold."

Then: "You want dessert? I'm counting to ten. ONE..."

That did it. We all ran home. Who was going to miss out on dessert?

My mother was a horrible cook. But my meal was nutritionally balanced. A green wad: vegetables. White spillage: potatoes. And a brown brick: meat. But all I wanted was my dessert. Devil Dogs: two soft layers of dark chocolate cake stuffed with white fluffy cream. Dee-lish!

My knowledge of people began at an early age, when I first began observing my mother's interactions with other people. She had barely made it out of high school, but her emotional IQ rivalled Einstein. Our apartment was always occupied, the coffee pot ever perking as neighbors, delivery men, friends all stopped in to chat, seek my mother's advice, or just have a laugh.

My mother listened intently to each individual, as if everything they shared was of the utmost importance. And each responded with grateful warmth. I watched carefully and tried to learn my mother's skills. I was able to make friends easily because of what I learned from her, but being the smallest kid on the block, I knew I would eventually have to deal with bullies. I was determined, no matter what, to never be a victim.

My first encounter with a bully was with a fifteen-year-old boy named Billy. I think I was about nine when I first encountered him.

All of us kids played in a park three blocks away: we used the swings, the basketballs, the handball courts. None of us had bikes or anything other than Spalding balls to throw around. So we made up our own games and rules, assigned roles for cops and robbers. We had a great time together, but one day, when we went to the park to use the swings, there sat Billy. Instead of playing with the boys on the basketball court, Billy swung on the swings, but he never interacted with us.

There were ten swings in all—a single long row—and Billy commandeered Swing #10 for himself. That was bad enough, but he also took over Swing #9 right next to him and kept it empty. Was that to prove what a big shot he was, or a strategy to keep us away from him so he wouldn't get girl cooties from us?

The swings were in a separate area enclosed by a chain link fence. We all lined up waiting our turn to take off into the sky. Somehow, without clocks or watches, we knew when it was time to vacate the seat and let the next person have it. We could then go back to the end of the line and await another turn. This arrangement wasn't as bad as it seems, because while waiting, we made jokes, teased each other affectionately, and made new friends.

But Billy never got on the line, never spoke to anyone…he just scared the crap out of us. One day I explained the Billy situation to my mother. She thought it over then said: "The only people who hurt others are those that are hurt themselves."

Sounds like one of those trite quotes from a magazine or a TV show. But the power of that one sentence changed my life in many ways, and it changed the lives of patients I worked with in the years ahead.

I decided to try out the insight I'd gained from my mother to see if she was right. Every time I went to the swing area, I stopped for a moment and looked through the chain-link fence at Billy on Swing #10 and his imaginary friend on Swing #9. Knowing Billy must be hurt inside, I'd smile at him and say, "Hi, Billy." Sometimes I'd add, "How are you today?" All spoken with the friendly warm smile I'd learned from my mother.

No verbal response from Billy. Instead, I'd get a look as if I'd just landed from Mars. Occasionally, I'd get a grunt in return. But never did a word pass between us, never a nod, and no acknowledgment other than a grunt.

For weeks, I kept up the same routine: smile, "Hi, Billy. How are you?" Then I'd enter the swing area and get on line with the rest of the girls.

One day something momentous happened…Billy wasn't there. The cheering, the hugs, the leaps in the air, outdid any Coney Island Fourth of July fireworks celebration. We took turns on Billy's two swings, congratulating each other and showing off our best moves.

A week went by and no Billy.

Maybe this was it: we had taken the land that was originally ours back from the tyrannical king.

Part of me wondered what had happened to Billy. But those feelings were tamped down by the joy and elation I shared with my friends. Then, almost two weeks later, Billy was back. I was made aware of his return by the muffled conversations I heard before I even arrived at the swing area. I approached the chain-link fence and looked at him.

"Hi, Billy…How are you? Are you all right? I missed you."

I had no idea why I said that last line, it just flew out of me uncensored. And then, as usual, no response from Billy. So I walked to the back of the swing line.

Suddenly, the ground erupted. It was as if King Kong had jumped from the Empire State Building and landed smack in the middle of the playground. Billy had climbed off of his swing and stood up. Everyone froze. The silence was lethal…I understood I had overstepped my bounds with Billy. There was going to be a price to pay.

Billy pointed to the end of the line, where I stood, then beckoned me forward. Everyone turned to face me. We all knew what was coming. Should I run? My friends would be sympathetic, but I'd be branded a coward forever and unmercifully teased for the rest of my life. But stepping forward meant getting the shit beat out of me. I had to make a quick decision. I figured the beating was a one-time event; the lifetime of teasing would last forever.

So as everyone stood with bated breath, I moved forward. The equivalent of a dead girl walking. As I approached, Billy looked down on me, I looked up at him. I inhaled deeply to compose myself and vowed I would not cry.

And then, Billy pointed to the empty swing and gestured that I should sit there. I did not know if this was a ploy for me to lower my guard before the hammer was released. But it turned out it wasn't. We climbed onto the swings and swung back and forth together in silence. Every day thereafter, Billy indicated I should take the swing next to him.

Slowly over time, I talked to Billy. About my family, about my sister, about my parents. Eventually Billy told me about his drunken father: he beat both his mother and Billy himself on a regular basis. I understood, without a word being said, that the swings were Billy's escape, and that the empty swing next to Billy served as a wall between him and a violent world....

I can't put into words the profound honor I felt that Billy trusted me with his most vulnerable self. And I never betrayed his trust by sharing his secrets. The understanding of the trust Billy showed me carried into my professional life, where I often had to convince other people so different from myself that they could share their innermost secrets with me.

I thought my friends in Brooklyn would resent me for taking the empty swing each time I came to the park, but they were in awe. They asked me how I had accomplished my feat. I don't remember the exact words I said in response; although I was young, part of me understood that I had treated Billy like a worthwhile person despite his menacing exterior. In other words, I had validated the good part of him, the part of him he had kept hidden from view.

Not all bullies responded to the same treatment—I knew that. But now, knowing that all bullies felt badly about themselves, and that their aggressive behavior was a way to compensate for their inner self-doubts, I had a leg up. Humiliation, especially in front of another person, was their worst enemy.

So when a bully boy and his friend approached me one day soon after my epiphany— and they started teasing me in order to get me to react—I knew what I had to do. Didn't know if it would work, but needed to give it a try. If I was wrong, I knew I'd get beat up.

I stood firm and looked this new bully in the eye. Why didn't I just walk away? Because the same scenario would happen again somewhere down the road: either this guy, or some other bully, would approach me with ill intentions. I had to try out my theory.

The new bully and his friend smiled gleefully, as if they already knew the outcome and couldn't wait to share their celebratory congratulations.

I held my position, staring with as much rage and aggression as I could possibly muster. I hoped I looked like a crazed lunatic. For just a flash, I saw the bully's confidence waver. Perhaps the situation might not turn out exactly as he had planned. Imagine the embarrassment in front of his lackey. He pushed my shoulder slightly. I did not respond. I stared back and said, "You're not from this block, are you?"

"So what?

"Let me tell you the rules," I said.

They both cracked up, laughing at the absurdity of the statement, as if we were engaging in an Olympic sport overseen by referees.

"Go ahead, tell me the rules," the bully said in a high-pitched voice, doing his best imitation of a girl.

I continued: "You want to fight, fine. But here, the fight doesn't end until one of us is dead."

The two intimidators got hysterical until I moved forward more aggressively.

"So you have to hit me first," I continued, "then if it's me that wins, I can claim self-defense when the cops come."

I moved forward again, staring into the boy's eyes and ignoring his friend. The friend moved back a bit, and the bully's confidence seemed to wane.

You know those Mafia movies where some poor schmuck is about to get whacked? I did my best imitation of a killer stare-down.

"You see," I said, "I've been through this before and I'm still here, and by the time I'm done with you, your balls will be cut off and shoved halfway down your throat until you choke to death."

I again moved a bit closer, still menacing, hoping I'd win an Academy Award for my first acting performance. After all, my well-being depended on it. The bully had to decide if I was bluffing or not. Could he take the chance of being humiliated by a girl in front of his best pal? I waited, he waited.

Finally, he burst into laughter. I remained still. His laugh ramped up into an explosion, which migrated over to his friend.

"You're crazy, you know that," he said. Then to his pal: "Let's go. This bitch is a total nut case."

They left. I breathed a sigh of relief. At least I now had another weapon in my bully arsenal. But there are times, when no matter how fast you think on your feet, events unfold with record speed and backup needs to be called.

My sister, Sarah, was six years older than me and seven inches taller when we reached adult height. One day I asked her, "How come we look so different?"

"Because you're adopted," she said.

I guess that's what older sister's do…they tease the younger ones. Our age gap was problematic at times. Sarah certainly didn't want to be around me and my half-grown friends, and I, well, all I wanted to do was run outside and play: stickball, tag, hide-and-seek, cops and robbers. I couldn't care less about her gossiping cohorts, or their analysis of the boys in their class, movie stars they had crushes on, then makeup and hairdos, and on and on.

And then Frederick came along. "'Frederick,' hey," he informed us, "it's *Frederick*, not *Freddy*, not *Fred*, got that?" Yeah, yeah, we all got it. He, Frederick, lived at the end of the block. He had no real interactions with the rest of us—other than reminding us to call him Frederick—so we ignored him. If I passed him on the block, I'd give him a weak smile and keep on going. Unlike with Billy, I had no need to engage with Frederick.

One day as I was coming home after having had an egg cream at the neighborhood candy store, I spied Frederick coming toward me. As he approached, I gave my usual half smile and started to move past him. My progress was halted by an unanticipated hard blow to my gut. Then Frederick kept walking. No words had passed between us, and now I was doubled over in pain, and slightly in shock. I couldn't breathe. My diaphragm felt paralyzed. The egg cream I'd just ingested spewed over the sidewalk. I couldn't speak, couldn't move, couldn't inhale. I *knew* I was going to die.

I remained bent over as if someone had folded me in two. After a while, a little breath came back and I tried to get to my apartment. But it was not to be. I collapsed halfway up the stairs. My sister must have heard the noise: she opened the door, took one look, then carried me up the stairs and placed me on the bed.

Sarah asked me what had happened, but I had no ability to answer her. And so we sat, I don't know for how long, and then she asked again if I could speak? I shook my head no. She brought me a glass of water and held it to my lips so I could sip slowly. Finally, I inhaled normally and she asked again, "What happened?"

"I was walking home, I passed Frederick, and out of nowhere, he punched me in the stomach."

"Just like that?"

"Just like that. He didn't say anything, I didn't say anything. I even smiled at him."

"Are you okay now?"

I nodded and continued to sip my water. My sister stood up, looked at me, then said, "I'll be back in a minute."

"Where are you going?"

Before the words were out of my mouth, she was gone. I heard her heavy footsteps run down the stairs. It must have been ten, I don't know, maybe fifteen minutes before I heard her footsteps returning. Sarah entered the bedroom, her breath as jagged as mine, her face bright red.

"Don't worry, Frederick will never bother you again," she said.

"What did you do?" I asked.

In the most matter-of-fact tone I'd ever heard, she said, "I grabbed his head and bashed it into the curb until he bled. Then I told him that if he ever laid a hand on you again I would kill him."

I looked into my sister's eyes and knew she meant it. And in that stunning moment, I realized I had a big sister. Not the taller, older, more sophisticated kind, but someone who would be there for me forever.

One of Sarah's friends knew a boy who studied self-defense. She had him come over and show me several moves a person my size could use to defend herself. To this day, I still know how to break away from someone strangling me, which areas of the body are most vulnerable to a kick or a hard hit that will disable an attacker and buy time to escape. Sarah's friend also taught me how to run through my defense options quickly.

So thank you, Frederick. As fucked up as you were and probably still are, I will be forever grateful. Sarah became my lifelong best friend. I shared everything with her: my hopes, dreams, failures, disappointments, the ups and downs of relationships. Even if I wronged someone, she always took my side. It was as close as I ever got to unconditional love, and I cherished it to the end.

I was now able to categorize bullies, and once I made my diagnosis, I knew how to handle them.

I was learning the language of the unspoken: reading others, seeing beyond the public facades, and acquiring an ability to relate to other people who were different from myself. Like Billy who occupied the swings.

I categorized the bullies I had met so far into three categories.

Bullies

Type #1—Defensive Bullies

These bullies include Billy, the swing magnate. Dealing with a difficult, unsafe situation at home, he silently placed a wall of intimidation between himself and others. Most importantly, he was not violent and secretly longed for a caring connection.

Type #2— The Intimidators

These bullies include the two boys who confronted me on the street, teasing, baiting, wanting me to be upset so they could prove their superiority to themselves.

Type #3—Violent without Feeling

These bullies include Frederick, who punched me in the stomach. Perpetrators and victims all emit an unspoken essence.

Years ago I watched a training film in which four men who had repeatedly mugged people on the streets were asked separately to watch a film of people walking down a sidewalk and to choose a victim. The walkers were of all types: a teenager, an elderly woman using a cane, a young woman in her twenties, various ethnic groups, a man in business attire, some in casual dress. I was astonished when all four of the perpetrators picked out the same two potential victims. No, not the elderly woman with the cane, or the young girl. It was the woman in her twenties and the man in the business suit. Why them? I wondered. They seemed the least likely targets to me.

But when the muggers explained their choice, it made sense. They had each perceived certain distinct traits in their chosen victims. Those targeted seemed unaware of their surroundings; they seemed meeker, almost frightened of interacting with others. The muggers knew they would not fight back. On the other hand, the elderly woman, whom I at first thought most muggers would have picked, had yelled at a passerby who accidentally knocked into her. Imagine what she could have done wielding her cane as a weapon.

Another time years ago, I was enjoying a day at the beach with two friends. After a while I decided to go for a walk alone along the shore. When

I returned from my walk, one of my friends commented, "You walk with a lot of assertiveness."

Huh? I thought. I'd never evaluated my walk, but subconsciously, I'd developed the walk of a non-victim.

We all deal with bullies as kids. So what? Later in life, as adults, these same individuals—bullies who have not worked out their underlying issues—might continue their assertive behavior in disguised form. Here's an example: A new supervisor once took over as head of the counseling department at one of the clinics where I worked. I'll call the supervisor The Boss. He probably would have loved this moniker as he did everything in his power to establish his dominance (see Bully #2, The Intimidator.)

Each week the staff at the clinic handed in notes detailing the progress our patients had made so the supervisor would be up-to-date in case any issues with our patients arose. The notes also provided other staff the information they would need if one of us called in sick, or was out on vacation, or had left the job. The notes were written quickly and efficiently as we all had a large caseload and prioritized our patients over writing our progress notes.

The progress notes were never intended to win a Pulitzer Prize. Misspellings, incorrect commas, were overlooked. The only important issues: the diagnosis, the treatment plan, the progress report.

Suddenly, one day The Boss marked up our reports with red ink, focusing on ridiculous issues, such as punctuation instead of the patients' well-being. Then I found out that most of The Boss's red marks appeared on the reports by female staff members, not on the men's reports.

I couldn't get in my "Boss's" face like I had those boys on the street. But now, knowing the type, I came up with a different plan. I walked into The Boss's office and said, "I got your corrections on my progress notes."

His self-satisfied smile told me everything I needed to know.

"I'd love to get better at my reports, can we sit and go over your comments?"

"Of course," he said beaming with pride.

I went over each mark on the paper. I asked a zillion questions. I kept this up for over an hour, watching The Boss's frustration build as I stole time from his precious day. Finally, at the end, I turned the tables on him. "Thank you so much," I said. "You've been so helpful. Can't wait until the next report. I have so much more to learn from you."

I smiled sweetly as I left—and that was my last report with red ink stains. And I still smile when I ask myself: Which of us became the dominant player in that situation?

THE UNEXPECTED

Given all the new insights and skills I'd gained by the age of twelve, I naively thought I was prepared for anything that could happen to me.

My heart was light as I stepped outside into a beautiful morning filled with fresh air, sunshine, and no school because it was Saturday. The only problem…no one to play with.

Everyone had taken the subway to the beach at Coney Island. My father was in synagogue, so no beach for us. I played stoopball, handball, jacks, all alone until finally Gordy appeared. He was the nephew of the superintendent from the apartment building next door. They had recently moved here from a Scandinavian country.

Even though Gordy was a lot older than me and my friends, about sixteen or seventeen, we had already accepted him into our play group. He helped out by retrieving balls, stopping traffic when we had to run into the street, giving us a leg up when we needed to climb a tree and get to our lookout post. The neighbors appreciated him doing miscellaneous chores: he never asked for money.

The minute Gordy appeared, I threw my ball at him, hoping to catch him off guard so we could share a laugh. But he grabbed the ball in midair as it was soaring over his head. And so our day began. We played games continually until we heard the jingle of Benny, the ice-cream man. *Yes!*

Gordy treated me to a chocolate crunch pop. He bought a vanilla for himself, and we sat on the stoop, licking our treats, talking in a muffled manner as the ice cream dripped down our cheeks, its coatings sticking to our tongues. After downing our treasures, Gordy suggested we play hide-and-seek. Before I could answer, he jumped up and ran down the alleyway where we usually played and disappeared. I raced after him, confident I would soon find him, as I knew all of the hiding places there. But Gordy was nowhere to be found. *Hmm…Sneaky, Gordy!* But I would figure it out.

Then, out of nowhere, Gordy jumped from behind a garbage can, startling me. Before I could react, he picked me up, put me over his shoulder, and carried me deeper into the alleyway, away from the view of all of the windows. I laughed. Gordy had outfoxed me.

Suddenly, he stopped and slammed me into the wall of the building, rattling my brain. I couldn't comprehend what was going on. He had me pinned against the wall unable to move. I looked up at his smile, which was half human, half animal. His breathing was like that of a mangy dog, and there was a wild look in his eyes. Was this the same Gordy we'd all played with for months? A member of our block? I didn't know him anymore, and I was scared.

As he unzipped his pants, a peculiar odor wafted upward. He exposed his erect penis and rubbed it against me. Then, his open hands crawled up the front of my body to grab hold of my blossoming breasts, his breathing more ragged than before.

I tried to speak, but words were smothered by a forceful kiss on my lips. So I violently shook my head from side to side, forcing his mouth away.

"Stop it, Gordy, stop it!" No response. "*Please, Gordy, stop it!*"

His unbuckled pants dropped to the ground, followed by his under-wear as he leaned down, aiming his engorged member toward my mouth.

The need to get away was so strong, it reactivated my brain. I calculated the odds that I might somehow escape safely. I needed to loosen his hold on me, so I smiled warmly. He smiled back, confident I had acquiesced. Then, I gently placed my hands on his shoulders, righted my balance, and pushed him backwards as hard as I could. He now was kneeling, and his pants were down around his ankles: I knew I had the advantage. He fell backwards, and I took off as fast as I could, breathing heavily, crying, my heart racing. I did not look back to see if he was closing in on me, as I knew I would lose precious seconds. I got to my stoop, raced upstairs to our apartment, then literally fell into my mother's arms, sobbing.

My mother instinctively knew something bad had happened; she held me tightly, rubbing my back to soothe me, calming me down. Not knowing what was going on.

"Sweetheart, what happened?" she asked.

I said nothing.

"Sweetheart, you know you can tell me anything. Did you do something wrong? Did someone do something to you? Please tell me."

I said nothing.

"Whatever it is, you know I'll help you take care of it. And I promise I won't be mad."

I tried with all of my might not to say a word, but finally the words came gushing forth.

I don't know if it made any sense, and I did not look at her face, afraid of seeing revulsion and disappointment in her eyes. She took hold of my shoulders, then gently moved my chin toward her. I felt her body shaking. Had I traumatized her too?

"I want you to know, that no matter what you may think at this moment, you did absolutely nothing wrong. *Nothing!* There's something wrong with Gordy, and he needs help. You are my wonderful child and always will be, and I love you *so* much."

"But I let him buy me ice cream. I went down the alleyway with him."

"I bet all the kids would have done the same thing," my mother replied. "Even the parents would have turned a blind eye. No one, not one person knew he was capable of this. He's sick in the head. Now, go rest awhile. Call me if you need me."

I went to my room, grateful for the respite. Before long I heard my father return home. Shortly thereafter, the cops arrived. They were the neighborhood police who knew all of us. And we knew and trusted them. I was never questioned, but a few days later, I asked my mother what had happened to Gordy.

"He was sent back home to his country."

Was that the truth? Or did she not want me to feel more guilt hearing that he was in jail?

I lost my innocence the day Gordy carried me down the alleyway and sexually assaulted me. I lost my faith in others, that feeling of safety that to this day has never fully returned. Gordy was a friend, he was one of us. I realized at that point that anyone could turn. That there were sides to people that could remain disguised behind smiles and generosity.

That knowledge has been profoundly insightful in helping me deal with criminals and their victims throughout my career.

I understood both sides of the scenarios: the guilt, confusion and trauma of the survivors, and the hidden dark pockets of evil within the souls of the perpetrators who commit such crimes. I had inherited a skill I would use many times throughout my career. I just wish I hadn't learned so much at the age of twelve.

THE ADVANTAGES OF
BEING A SQUIRREL

Several years after recovering, with my mother's help, from the trauma I experienced as a result of Gordy's assault, I was ready to start my dating life.

I was in high school by then, already a wise, sophisticated woman, having been married at the age of five. No, it wasn't a sex-slave operation. A neighborhood boy asked me to marry him and showed me the plastic ring he'd gotten as a prize from a Cracker Jack box. What girl refuses jewelry? So we had a little ceremony in someone's backyard. I kept the ring and dumped the boy. Yes, I started my dating life as a real bitch.

When I got to high school, I thought my short stature would be an impediment to dating, but the opposite happened. To this day I still do not understand it.

My father was a smidge taller than six feet, and my mother was a smidge taller than five feet. My uncle was six feet on the nose, and his wife was a tad under five feet. What is it with tall guys hooking up with small women?

One day I was standing in line at a bank, chatting with a guy who was nearly six-and-a-half-feet tall. After we finished our banking business, the man asked me out for coffee. As we walked down the street, we looked like a giraffe and a squirrel heading to the local diner. I *wished* I was a squirrel, that way I could have climbed up his body and gone eye to eye with him. By the time the walk was done, I needed a chiropractor to crack my neck back into place.

Little did I know how useful my small stature would be while working in the locked facilities of a psychiatric prison, or on the locked ward of an all-male thirty-day detox hospital; both places filled with patients experiencing anxiety and volatility for the entire length of their commitment.

I was obviously no physical threat to the patients: if one of them sneezed forcefully enough, I would have landed on my ass. But they appreciated the fact that I had chosen to try and help them in situations that sometimes turned dangerous. Meanwhile, another part of my body became a diagnostic tool, separating the guys I wanted to date from those I did not.

My looks were average, nothing special. But I learned early on, especially by watching my mother who was no great beauty either, that on the dating scene, personality and an ability to relate to others were just as valuable as looks. And as looks lagged later in life, those with people smarts, only got better with age, like a fine wine.

Just as valuable on the high school dating landscape were breasts: the bigger the better. They dazzled boys like a magnet in a steel factory.

I don't know where my voluminous beauties came from. My mother's bra size was a B cup; my sister, who was seven inches taller than me, had a D cup. On her body that made sense. But on my small frame, I had two watermelons protruding from my chest that could have knocked over a herd of buffaloes. I stuffed these appendages into a C cup even though I knew I needed a larger size. I saw how boys acted when confronted with breasts. That's all they focused on, not the eyes, not the face, just the boobs. That's not what I wanted, so I wore a large size blouse and an oversized sweater when

I went to parties. I'd sit, wait, and observe until inevitably a girl would enter wearing a blouse one size too small, showing cleavage down to her belly button. Then I'd watch the boys salivate and race over to gain her attention, their testosterone flying in every direction. Once the herd thinned, I looked for the boys still seated and went to speak with them. Not all of them were a good match, but many turned out to be fun, enjoyable dates: boys who provided laughter and good conversation, boys who looked into your eyes, not at your knockers.

When I entered high school, I had heard that each grade put on a big show at the end of the year. The show was the main event at school, the excitement building until the last month of school. The annual show included skits about the school, jokes about the teachers, and lyrics set to current popular songs. I immediately signed up.

I loved being part of live theater. I think it reminded me of growing up on the block where we made up our own games, characters, dialogue, in a collaborative process where everyone was treated as an equal. Every element of putting on a show became part of a single organism that had to be perfectly attuned to its surroundings or the whole thing would go down the tubes. Props, costumes, set building, set changes, lighting, music cues, directing, acting in front of a live audience. Each one dependent upon the other.

As I'm sure everyone who ever went to high school knows, there is a hierarchy among the students: pretty girls and athletes on top, everyone else juggling for position. Whatever happened to brains, heart, and kindness leading the way?

Having been blessed with Jewish-girl looks, I knew I would not rise to the top of the food chain. Have you ever seen a picture of Albert Einstein? I used to joke that God had to compensate Einstein for his Jewish looks so he gave him a genius brain.

When I joined the annual high school show each year, I loved it. I made new friends, and I realized that I'd developed some creative skills as a result of playing on the block back in Brooklyn. I wrote skits and created song lyrics to accompany the musical sections of the script. All of a sudden, the "pretty girls" acknowledged me in the hallways. The interactions were small, trite, but I was never snubbed. Creating together was an avenue toward equalizing relationships.

So all went well in high school. I had the annual show, I had some new friends, my grades were good, and I'd started dating. What could possibly happen? I'd survived bullies, a sexual assault, could now read other's intentions. I was a survivor!

But I was also young, too young to understand the ever-changing roller coaster of life. I bought my ticket to the ride, anticipating the joy that was about to follow.

And then, in my junior year, the bottom dropped out of my life. No, let me be more truthful...It was as if I had fallen down an elevator shaft, unable to scream for help. And even if I had screamed for someone to come to my rescue, those who could have saved me had enough trouble saving themselves.

THE DEEP DIVE

My family unit was changing. My aunt had married a very rich man, and she provided funds for my sister to head off to college in the Midwest. As I was now old enough to care for myself, my mother decided to go back to work rather than become an empty nester. She obtained a secretarial job in Manhattan and loved the camaraderie, being involved with different age groups, making friends, and having a new sense of purpose.

Around this time, in the middle of my junior year at high school, I came home from school one day to find my father waiting for me. In the middle of a work day? The last time that had happened, Gordy had sexually assaulted me. So I knew something bad had gone down.

"Mom is in the hospital," my father said.

I looked at him. "What? What are you talking about?"

"She collapsed on the subway."

That didn't sound too bad. The subways were hot; sometimes people fainted. I wasn't too alarmed.

We went into Manhattan to see her, and she seemed fine. In fact, she was holding court from her bedside, just as she had done in our kitchen throughout my childhood. Nurses passing in the hallway, aides, janitors, other patients and their families all stopped by for a visit and a laugh. She still knew how to entertain, even if her costume was now a dull-colored over-sized hospital gown.

My father and I left the hospital that evening after visiting hours. I had a peaceful night's sleep knowing our lives would soon return to normal. But I came home the next day after school, and there was my father waiting for me again. No, my mother hadn't died, but as awful as this is to say, over the next year and a half, I kept wishing she had, for what ensued was worse than death.

My loving, sweet, gentle, social butterfly of a mother had incurable brain cancer.

The disease took its time devouring her, and every change in her, both physically and psychologically, was worse than Frederick's gut punch to my stomach. And this time, my sister could not bash anyone's head on the side-walk to stop the ongoing assault.

When my mother returned from the hospital, after several days, things were good at first. My father resumed his typical work schedule, I continued high school, my sister was still away at college; the only change, my mother did not return to work. With the financial help of my wealthy aunt, an aide was hired during my school hours; I took over after school until my father returned from work, then I went into my room to do homework.

I was now in my senior year in high school, and while most kids were dating, some going "all the way" sexually, experimenting with cigarettes and pot, my life was consumed with my mother and her needs.

I heard from my friends of all of their newfound adventures as I sat watching my mother deteriorate. She was in pain, but tried hard to hide it from me. Hospice care and palliative treatments were not widely available back then. At times she would send me to the kitchen to fetch water for her, but I could hear her groaning, trying to stifle the sounds beneath her pillow. At other times, she was slipping away.

"Mom, are you all right?" I'd ask as I saw her drift off.

"I'm fine, sweetheart," she'd reply, "don't worry about me."

I did my best to amuse her, making up skits, both of us laughing together. We still hugged and enjoyed each other's company. Then, we reached a tipping point, and my mother's health headed downhill rather quickly. She had trouble keeping her balance, she would walk into walls. I had to stand behind her, my hands under her arms, to steer her to and from the bathroom.

Her appearance changed dramatically. She lost most of her weight and all of her hair. She had to be fed by hand. The smell of her body rotting from the inside permeated her room, adding to the mounting indignities.

I came home from school one day, the aide left, and I took over as usual. I walked into my mother's bedroom, said, "Hi, Mom," and gave her a hug. She always hugged me back, but not this time. I looked into her eyes and saw the confused look on her face. Who the hell was I? She had no idea.

The woman who had raised me, who looked after me, who laughed with me and guided me past life's stumbling blocks, was no longer present. Then a glimmer of hope: she reached out and caressed my cheek; but it wasn't with love or recognition, she was using her sense of touch to figure out who I was.

"Mom, it's me…your daughter."

She smiled at me, but it was the same smile she bestowed on people she'd just met.

Her last night on Earth was hell. She had nonstop seizures, shaking, unable to speak, completely betrayed by her own body. We called an ambulance and took her to the hospital, where the staff administered drugs to stop the seizures. Then the doctor said I could see her alone.

I walked into her room and saw a tortured, sedated creature lying in a hospital bed: bald skeleton, skin now yellowed from jaundice, my mother's bones protruding out of her body. This was her reward for living a life of kindness, caring for others, lifting their spirits, letting them know she could see the person inside, and that each person she saw was special.

We held a funeral the next day, early spring blossoming all around. I fainted while the rabbi was speaking. My uncle had to carry me from the funeral home to the parking lot outside to get a breath of fresh air. I don't remember much else. A few weeks later, a charity was scheduled to come to my parents' home to pick up a donation of my mother's clothes. As I was preparing for the pickup, I stood inside her closet and inhaled her scent. Then, I wrapped the arms of her favorite sweater around my shoulders. That was the last time my mother held me.

Each of us has themes that attach to us throughout our lives. Mine were now established: abandonment and anxiety.

I had overcome the bullies, the sexual assault by Gordy, with the aid and wisdom of my mother. But who would help me now to get through the worst blow of all?

I plunged into a deep depression. A black hole of anonymity with no connection to the outside world. And yes, I fantasized about suicide.

If there was an afterlife, I knew my mother was looking down on me; how could I allow my death be her legacy? She had given me so much! At the time, I did not know how useful my gains would be when aiding other people whom I had yet to meet, but whose lives would eventually cross mine.

And so I began my struggle out of the black hole, one slow step at a time, sliding backwards at every holiday, every birthday celebration when I saw an empty chair beside us at the table.

When I think about the struggles of watching my mother die—the emotional and psychological battles I waged while coming back from the brink of suicide—I realized I had more strength than I had ever imagined. And if I needed that strength again, even under horrible circumstances, I now knew I could be there for others.

BACKWARDS, FORWARDS

After my mother died, I had a few free weeks over the summer before I started college. But I did nothing, saw no one, went nowhere.

I looked around my home, our apartment, at photographs of family vacations, trips to Coney Island, where my elation stood in the forefront as I held up a stuffed animal I'd won playing Skee-Ball. Various photographs of my sister growing from a child to a woman, my mother laughing with friends, both my parents dressed up for some special occasion. And there, in the center of the collage: me as an infant being snuggled in my mother's lap, my sister's arm around me. All monuments of our time together, our family's innocence. As much as I wanted to remain within that cocoon, time would not allow it, college was around the corner.

Most of my friends were going to attend college in Brooklyn, but I needed to get away. My feelings were still that raw. So I applied to a college in Manhattan and was accepted. Still, how would I make new friends, the walls of loss still so thick around me? I chose theater as my major, with a double minor in psychology and sociology.

Was my choice a practical combination for a career? No it wasn't, but it was a good choice for my mental health. The old me emerged fueled by inspiration and aspiration, new friends and mind-expanding courses. I breathed deeply, hopeful that given a little more time, I would be all right. And then the next blow.

One day I came home during my first year in college, to find that my father wanted to talk with me. Never a good sign.

"I'm seeing…I guess *dating* a friend of a friend."

"What?" I said. "Who? How?"

"Her name is Miriam."

"I don't remember any 'Miriam.'"

"One of the friends from the monthly poker game introduced us. She recently lost her husband."

"So you're forming a relationship out of loss?" That was not very empathetic on my part.

My father said, "We'll talk about this another time." And with that, he left the room.

How could he, after only a few months, find another woman? Or was he so devastated by the loss of my mother that "Miriam" became his fix? I called my favorite member of the family, Aunt Betty, my father's youngest sister.

"Of course he loved your mother," she said, "they were childhood sweethearts. Who wouldn't love your mother? But you have to remember, he's lived his whole life taking care of others. All of us as kids after our father died," she explained, "then you, your sister, and your mother. What does he do now? Sarah's an adult, you'll soon be on your own. He's never been alone in his life."

I sort of understood and decided I would make the best of it for my father's sake, even though…well, when I met Miriam, she wasn't exactly my kind of person. Then, before I could adjust, out of nowhere, they were getting married.

That was upsetting, but not as horrific as coming home one day after school and finding my mother wiped off the face of the Earth. All traces of her were gone: the photographs, her favorite knickknacks, even the coffee pot that kept the social life of the neighborhood flowing. Neither of them asked me if I wanted any photograph or keepsake. To this day, I have only three photographs of my past. That's it. Everything else wiped away as if it never existed!

But, on the plus side, I now had permission to lead a whole new life for myself. I even started dating again, something I hadn't done in the last year and a half. I was behind in the "virginity" department, if you know what I mean, and decided I had to make up for lost time.

It would have to be someone special; after all, I had only one gift to give, and the experience had to last a lifetime. After going to many parties, meeting new people, I finally met "the one" at a frat party. Donny. He had that male essence I was attracted to: a confidence in himself, his future, his intelligence (he was a physics major in his senior year of college), and most of all, a sense of humor.

We started dating, and then it happened: I was consumed by my desire for him. I thought about him all day, couldn't wait to hear his voice on the phone, feel his touch, and inhale his masculine scent. This was supposed to be just about sex, remember? Maybe it was also about that empty space inside that only the touch and intimacy of another human being could fill. Whatever it was, I was all in.

I knew it was time, and so did Donny. Don't worry, nothing pornographic is coming up, just hilarity. While others had their first experience encased in a great romantic story, I wound up living mine as a character in a farce. Ah, but where do we do the deed? Although my father was at work during the day, you-know-who occupied the apartment while he was gone.

Thankfully, Donny said his apartment, where he lived with his parents, would work. His mother and father were on vacation for several days, and his older sister lived and worked in another borough of the city. We were all set for the special event on a Friday afternoon. The moment arrived, we were both giddy with anticipation.

We entered Donny's apartment laughing, teasing, and immediately started flinging our clothes all over the living room like some scene from a popular rom-com. Finally, we arrived at his bedroom, both totally naked; together we crawled under the covers for the big event.

Knowing it was my first time, Donny was very sweet and considerate, careful to check that I was comfortable with each of his chosen activities. As the curtain was about to go up on Act 1, we heard the front door slam shut. Someone was in the apartment! A burglar? I scanned the room for possible weapons in case Donny and I had to fight our way out of the situation. I figured our nakedness would be a surprise to the interloper and give us an edge for a few seconds before the perpetrator made his first move.

Then, a female voice called out:

"Donny, Donny, are you home?"

Who the hell was this? A girlfriend he hadn't told me about? I turned to Donny with anger and fear in my eyes. Then he whispered:

"That's my sister. She's supposed to be at work!"

Oy vey! I did not want to meet his sister for the first time clad in my birthday suit. But my clothes were strewn around the living room, no way to retrieve them without exposing myself in my full regalia. What if she saw the clothes and….Well, I'm sorry, but I couldn't help it: my panic was replaced by waves of laughter. Donny put his fingers to his lips to shush me, and I buried my head under a pillow to let loose there. Then Donny yelled out:

"I'm sick. Some kind of food poisoning. I just want to sleep."

"I'll make you some soup," Donny's sister responded.

Her voice sounded the same as when she first entered, so I figured she hadn't seen the clothes tossed around the living room yet.

"What are you doing here in the afternoon?" he yelled out.

"It's Friday, summer hours, we get out early. I thought I'd stop by for a visit. How about I make you some tea?" she asked. "I'm having some myself."

Oh, God, she was about to make herself comfortable in the kitchen and have her afternoon tea. Did she bring scones with her? How long would I be buried, naked, hiding under blankets with my head muffled in a pillow? What if I had to pee?

"Listen," Donny yelled, "I'm going to have explosive diarrhea soon. I don't want you here when it happens. Could you please leave?"

Great come back, Donny!

Then—complete silence. We waited, perfectly still.

Donny tried to imitate a huge fart to further enhance his story, but it only made me laugh more. Nothing like sound effects to prop up the story. Finally, we heard the apartment door open and slam shut. Had she been insulted by his tone and left? Had she seen the strewn clothes in the living room…or had the explosive diarrhea and humongous fart frightened her off?

I never found out, because apparently Donny and his sister never discussed the incident. Needless to say, we set another day for the big event, and not on a Friday, when Donny's sister might make another appearance. The next time went off as planned, but I have to admit, I did miss a little bit of the excitement the first time held even with our unwanted guest.

I had fallen in love with Donny, and I told him so. I really wanted the relationship to work out.

But, at the end of Donny's senior year, the relationship ended. Donny was off to graduate school across the country, and I got dumped. And yes, it sent me into another tailspin fueled by loss, abandonment, and depression. I vowed I would never love anyone deeply again. And I kept my promise through my next series of relationships.

ON MY OWN

What is home? A place where you eat, sleep, shower. Is that it? If so, then I guess I had a home with my father and Miriam. But if the definition includes warmth, love, emotional safety, then I was homeless.

Miriam and I could not get past our suspicions of each other, each waiting for the other's move on a hostile chessboard. I worried Miriam would say something negative about my mother, and she worried that she would never have full possession of the apartment—or my father—while my presence and past permeated the atmosphere.

And so, during my last term of college, I took all the money I'd earned at my office temp jobs and moved to a furnished apartment in a fourth-floor walkup. Was I happy? No. Was I free? Yes, in a sense.

I was now an adult, responsible for myself, in need of money. Thus, my first fulltime job at the drug detox hospital, serving tuna salad during my interview.

At the time, dress code for women meant a skirt or a dress. What? No one could tell I was a girl if I wore pants? I was assigned to an all-male unit. I looked forward to interacting with the patients in the day room, speaking to them one-on-one in their rooms. And, unlike the counseling staff, I knew I would not be sitting behind a desk.

So I arrived on my first day of work excited to start my permanent job. I was partnered with Mark, who was over six feet tall, thin, and a lovely man. Again it looked like the giraffe and the squirrel meandering through the hallways. Mark was sweet, easy to talk to, and had a good sense of humor, an essential trait when working in places such as the detox hospital, where you're exposed to a host of trauma, tragedies, and other horrible life situations. But I was ready for my training. Only there wasn't any training. It was sink or swim. And perhaps living within that setting on a daily basis was the only way to determine whether one's personality was suited for that type of environment. And I have to say, I loved it!

No two days were ever the same. Our population turned over every thirty days, new personalities needing different interactions arrived, keeping the energy high and the adrenalin on alert.

Friends asked whether I was frightened working on a locked ward with detoxing men, some with violent pasts. And the answer was no.

For the first time in my life, my short stature became an asset. I did not provoke male dominance responses, as I was too short to threaten anyone. The patients instinctively understood that I had willingly put myself in a position to help them. And so they looked out for me. If a patient got out of control, the other patients made sure to form a protective barrier around me.

I learned to present myself to the patients with authority (not an authoritarian attitude) that commanded their attention when needed. But my greatest skill was learned during my childhood: how to relate to others. The more different a patient at the detox hospital was from me, the more I wanted to learn all about him: his thoughts, feelings, life perspective, and experiences. I was respectful to all of the patients. I didn't care what the patient had done on the outside, whatever crimes had been committed; I wanted to form a bond with the healthy person inside, just like I had done with Billy, the bully with his empty swing on the playground back in Brooklyn. In return, I hoped that the respect and genuine caring I showed to others, would be shown to me.

Anyone can identify a phony, or someone slogging through their job. Those who had lived on the streets, spent time in jail, lost their families, had a hyperacute sense of who is authentic and who isn't—and authenticity can be one's greatest asset in life. Over time I exchanged my nervous inside for a calm interior and the confidence that I could spontaneously handle whatever ensued.

The way the program worked, if a patient completed a month of detox, including counseling and medical care, he was allowed to return to the hospital pretty quickly if he had a relapse. Relapses are part of the process of leaving addiction behind. If a patient returned quickly, I knew he either had genuine motivation to change, or he needed to lower his drug usage and fly out the door again. If a patient did not complete the program and signed out against medical advice, a longer penalty period was enforced before the patient was allowed to return to the program. Some made it through and went on to have productive lives, others did not. Motivation, and sometimes hitting rock bottom, were necessary for real change to occur.

During the course of my job, I had to teach myself how to translate material that was often very complicated—but that I knew would help my patients—into every day conversation. I'm sorry if that sounds patronizing. But my rule of thumb was: no judgment, no big vocabulary. If I hadn't learned to use the same language the patients used, I would have alienated the very people I had come to help.

After a few months on the job, I'd finally gotten my new skill set down and no longer felt like a newbie. This was confirmed when one of the patients I knew when I had first started the job returned for treatment after a relapse.

"Boy, have you changed," he said.

I hadn't yet fully learned all the nuances of reading nonverbal behavior: body language, eye movement, tonal changes, speech hesitations, so I wondered whether the patient's new assessment of me was positive or negative.

"I'm not sure what you mean," I said, holding my breath, waiting for the hammer to fall and destroy my newfound abilities.

"You seem so confident, so calm," the patient explained. "When you first came here you were constantly looking around, wondering what was going on. Now, you know everything going on in the dayroom without turning your head."

I think that was the nicest compliment I ever received. Many women want to hear how pretty or sexy they are, but knowing I had conquered my anxieties and had a newfound sense-of-self was better than any compliment I could have been given. I was now a professional—and best of all, I felt like one.

I spoke easily with the patients, played games with them in the dayroom, intervened in disputes, listened as they trusted me with their innermost thoughts and feelings. Being out on the floor with them instead of in an office made our interactions more spontaneous and less intimidating. No door between us symbolizing the educated professional behind the barrier. And then I met Jackie.

JACKIE

Jackie was a combat veteran who served in Vietnam where he and many others became addicted to drugs as a way to cope with their hellish situation. One night, while working the evening shift, I heard screaming coming from his room.

A nurse and I rushed in to see what was happening. We found Jackie in the midst of a turbulent nightmare.

We gently roused him from sleep and waited until he reoriented himself. I offered to sit with him for a while, which he agreed to. He smiled at me to indicate that he was all right, but I knew he wasn't. As he eased back to the present time, I offered to play cards with him, which he gratefully accepted. As he relaxed, I put out a couple of feelers, trying to help him open up, but he didn't respond. It was the same experience I kept having over and over again with war veterans.

Once, when visiting a friend's house, I sat down to talk with the friend's father, who was a World War Two vet. He was part of an advance team that opened supply routes for soldiers entering the fray. Because they were an advance team, they were often attacked.

When I asked my friend's father about his experiences, he took me into his office and showed me "souvenirs" he had taken from dead Nazis' bodies. He never said whether he had killed them himself or had simply taken them from bodies he found along the way. He was not bragging about his exploits; in fact, the look in his eyes was the exact opposite, revealing trauma and deep sadness. When I tried to get him to be more specific, he shut down. I asked why none of the veterans would talk to me. Was it because they did not wish to relive the horror of war? His answer surprised me.

"I went over there to protect my country and keep my family from harm. Why would I put images in their head of what went on there? Images that they would never be able to get rid of. What kind of husband or father would I be if I did that to my family?"

I then realized how important all of the veterans' services are to those who sacrificed so much physically, mentally, and emotionally for the rest of us.

What I'm going to tell you certainly does not compare to the experiences of war veterans. But when working with others whose life experiences are so different from my own, I found it helpful to hook into something in my own life that had even the least little bit of resonance to their situation. Again, I'm only talking about myself now, and how I work. What I am about to share may seem trivial to some; no disrespect is intended to any war veteran, but what I'm about to tell you did help me hook into the silence of not sharing trauma with others.

SAMMY

While working at the outpatient methadone clinic later on in my career (the one where Michael aimed a knife at my throat), I met Audi and her husband Charles, a mother and father, both drug addicts, who brought their six-year-old boy, Sammy, with them when picking up their medication. They were doing well, and even though they were not assigned to my team, I looked forward to their visits. Sammy was a delight; adorable and charismatic…He brought a joyfulness to the staff and to the difficult lives of the other patients.

One day, one of the nurses came to my office in a panic.

"Did you hear what happened to Sammy?" the nurse said.

"No, what?"

"He's in the hospital, upstairs on peds. He's a mess."

We both ran upstairs. I found Sammy lying in bed, IVs hooked up, bandages wrapped around most of his body, a breathing tube down his throat. I thought I would faint.

The nurse on duty told us the boy had suffered severe abuse at the hands of his parents. *What?* As far as I and my colleagues at the clinic knew there had been no visible signs of abuse previously. I hadn't worked with Audi and Charles, but the team that knew the family were all extremely competent. Sammy had seemed well cared for and happy. I'd encountered child abuse in the past, and of course I had read about cases in the news and watched reports on TV. Neither Sammy nor his parents checked any of the boxes. When I was informed of the details regarding what his parents had actually done to him, I went into the bathroom and vomited. His recovery— if he ever *did* recover—would take years, not months; either way, multiple surgeries lay ahead of him.

But the worst part (the *worst* part!)…When I looked into his eyes, I knew Sammy was gone. The sweet, little, loving child no longer existed within his permanently disfigured body. The Sammy I knew was lost forever.

I went home and cried. Not just cried: I heaved sobs over and over again until I finally had no strength left and fell onto my bed. I couldn't sleep and called in sick the next day.

Eventually, I got my equilibrium back, and I returned to my normal routine. I understood then a little of what my friend's father had shared about not telling his family about his war experiences: to this day, I've never told anyone the details of what Sammy's parents had actually done to him and the prolonged torture Sammy must have experienced. The abuse was beyond anything I thought humans capable of perpetrating on a child—or on an adult, for that matter. Like my friend's father, I was not going to implant images of such inhuman, unfeeling, sadistic behavior in the minds of those I cared about.

Even today, stories of child abuse bring me back to Sammy, and I often cry and get depressed.

JINGLE BELLS AND TISSUES

Christmas was approaching. Time to hand out presents to the patients. What I expected to be a fairly routine activity turned out to be anything but ordinary.

The gifts were generic: gloves, socks, scarfs. Alan, one of the counselors who was going to play Santa Claus, asked me to be his elf. I was flattered until I realized hardly anyone else was small enough to fit into the elf costume. But what the heck, it was for the patients.

Alan and I practiced our greeting:

"Ho, Ho, Ho, Merry Christmas!" Alan boomed in his deep baritone voice.

"Ho, ho, ho, Merry Christmas," I squealed in a high-pitched, squeaky voice.

We began our deliveries on my unit, of course. My patients laughed at my costume and imitated my squeaky voice—not just that day, but for the whole week.

It was great fun, until we reached the women's unit. We walked into a quiet room, the nearest patient to the door lying in her bed, her eyes staring at the ceiling. We sang our joyous greeting, and I handed her a gift. Instead of taking it, she squeezed her two hands over mine and said, "Thank you. Thank you so much. I'm most grateful for the gift." Tears streamed down her cheeks, sadness and pain emanating from her eyes.

Then, I got it. Our patients were separated from their families at holiday time; more important, many of them had been thrown out of their homes, and often they were dismissed by their community because of their toxic drug abuse. The insight hit me hard when I went to a neighbor's party two months after I had started my job.

I saw a young man dressed in jeans, T-shirt, and sneakers. He was not trying to impress anyone, as some of the others were: they wore obviously expensive slacks and shirts, with flashy rings on their fingers.

I sat next to the least showy guy, and after the usual greetings, the common conversational opening began....

"So what kind of work do you do?" I asked.

"I'm in finance, evaluating stocks, doing technical analysis. And you?"

"I work as a recreational therapist in a thirty-day detox hospital," I said proudly.

"You work with drug addicts?" he said incredulously. I thought my answer had surprised him because of my size, until he added, "Well, I guess someone has to do that kind of work."

Without realizing it, he'd moved about six inches from me, as if my work might somehow be contagious. I stood up, looked him directly in the eyes and responded:

"Well, thank God it's not you."

And with that I took my leave.

THE MORON

At the detox hospital, The Moron was hired as a counselor, not because he exhibited the traits needed for the job, nor the desire to work at the detox hospital, and certainly not because he desired to learn new skills. How did he get hired? His uncle was an administrator at the hospital. Don't you just love nepotism? Later, after he did what he was about to do, I figured the Moron couldn't keep a job elsewhere, so why not throw him into our workplace because, as you already know by now, our patients do not rank very high on the ladder of human worth.

So what training did he have? None. Who supervised him? No one. Why? Because the Moron was so arrogant, he disagreed with anyone trying to train him. After all, his back was covered by his uncle. How nice.

Mark and I were working the evening shift—and that was mainly when the Moron worked. Perhaps they thought he would do the least amount of damage at night, but they didn't think about the fact that fewer staff were on duty after normal working hours.

The Moron worked in the counseling office. As you know, Mark and I were out on the floor with the patients at all times.

One night, after we returned from dinner, we unlocked the door to the ward and immediately knew there was trouble. We did not even have to walk down the hallway. We heard shouting and cursing…it felt like the whole place was ready to explode.

We looked at each other wondering if we should run and lock the door behind us, but it never dawned on either of us to actually flee the scene. Not merely because we were conscientious workers, but because these were our patients. We *knew* them. And right now, they needed us.

As we turned onto the hallway, all of the patients, dressed in hospital pajamas and robes, were standing in groups in the corridor. We heard them discussing which items could be used as weapons.

Weapons? I thought.

Even in a place like the detox hospital where there is a constant turn-over of patients, knowing which patient is most respected by the others is critical. Individuals who had earned the respect of their peers often helped us intervene in conflicts before any violence broke out. Unfortunately, the situation Mark and I encountered that night was already going full blast.

Henry, our most highly respected patient at the time, came over to Mark and me. Apparently, the Moron had lost his temper, got on the PA system, and belittled the patients for being addicts, being on welfare, committing crimes, etcetera, etcetera. His rant went on for several minutes.

As I look back, I still can't believe the Moron or anyone else would do something so stupid and inhumane in a treatment facility.

We thanked Henry for the information; then Mark and I went to a corner to confer. Our first priority was to make sure that no one got hurt; unfortunately, that included the Moron as well. If one person blew, the whole place would explode like a lit match in an ammunition factory. We needed to separate the patients so a crowd mentality would not suddenly arise, allowing the situation to get out of hand.

We asked Henry to help us get everybody back into their rooms, and we said that we would come around and talk to each person individually to hear them out.

Oh, by the way, the Moron was now safely locked inside an office. How nice for him. Our asses were now on the line, not his.

Henry and several other patients got everyone back into their rooms. I went to some of the patients' rooms, Mark went to others. We listened. We empathized.

"We're so sorry this happened," I told the patients I spoke to. "No one for any reason should ever speak to you with such disrespect."

I had to be patient and listen to each one as his rage spewed forth. Let everyone get as much out of his system as possible.

"Look, I'm as furious as you are," I told them. "But my concern now is for you."

They each looked up, thinking my concern would be for the Moron, whom they were going to beat the shit out of once he left his office. They were surprised by what I said next.

"If any violence goes down, who do you think will be blamed? It will be all of you. That's not fair but that's the way it will go down. Some of you are on parole, probation, have court cases pending. If the Moron"—I didn't call him that in front of the patients—"is hurt, you'll get the extra time. Is he worth it? Do you really want him to get away with this at your expense? What's the worst they'll do to him? Fire his ass? Think about what will happen to you. I promise that Mark and I will make sure the hospital knows what happened, and you'll never see or hear from him again. But I need your word, your absolute promise, that when we get him out of his office, no one will harm him."

And so it went, room after room after room. The same conversation. Then, to reinforce it all, Henry and a few others went back to each room to make sure the patients were all on the same page. When Henry assured us all was in place, Mark and I knocked on the door to the office where the Moron had secured himself, and the Moron himself let us in. We closed the door behind us.

I took one look at the Moron and saw he was scared shitless. That thrilled me. I have *never* lost my temper at work, no matter what has gone down, because it only leads to disaster. But here I was confronting the idiot who had put all of our lives in danger. I lost it. I guess I felt safe enough to let go inside a locked room.

"You fucking, stupid, asshole, moron." That was my opening salvo. "If you want to kill yourself that's your choice, but now you are endangering me, Mark, and everyone on the floor. Now I understand why you can't hold a job, because you–are–a–total–failure." I know how harsh that was, but to this day I don't feel guilty about it.

Mark then intervened, holding up his hand to stop my rant. "Here's what we're going to do," Mark said. "We are going to walk you down the hall—the patients have agreed not to hurt you—and we will take you off this unit. If you say anything, you can get us all killed. Do you understand?"

Then I jumped in again: "You are not to talk to the patients, you are not to look at the patients no matter what they say or do, and most of all—and I don't know if you're capable of this—keep your head down and try, even if you have to fake it, to show remorse. Are we clear?"

The Moron nodded. If he did not obey our instructions, forget the patients hurting him, I would beat the shit out of him myself. Mark and I then opened the counseling door, and Henry was waiting for us. We asked him whether the coast was clear, and he said yes. When we looked outside, we were greeted with a sight I did not expect. All of the patients were lined up on both sides of the corridor, their backs against the wall, facing the pathway we would have to walk down. Henry assured us it was okay. Was it? We wouldn't know until we stepped outside. What else could we do?

And so it began, Mark on one side of the Moron, me on the other. We headed slowly down the corridor. Both Mark and I smiled to the patients to let them know how appreciative we were to have their cooperation. Then, all of a sudden, they started spitting. We had no way to prepare; it was as if a flock of pigeons had flown overhead—but instead of shitting on us, they decided to spit on us. The spit was aimed at the Moron, but Mark and I got drenched in the process. If there was ever an Olympic event for forming the longest spit line, and spitting the farthest distance, our patients would have won the gold medal!

The three of us worked our way to the exit door, each of us soaked head to toe in a glorious river of saliva. And no, I never wore that outfit again. We did get the Moron off the unit, however. His career as a counselor was over. If anything can bond human beings together, it's working as a team during a crisis. Mark and I became good friends, and throughout my career some of my longest lasting friendships came from working with others at my unusual places of employment.

FIGHTING FOR DIGNITY

My jobs in a variety of settings often required me to fight for patients who could either not fight for themselves or were dismissed as unworthy by others. Either their mental illness interfered, or perhaps their lack of education, or their drug addiction, or a general inexperience dealing with professionals such as doctors, lawyers, managers.

On the first day of one of my courses in the school where I studied social work, one of my professors said something like, "The job of a bureaucracy is to keep the bureaucracy going."

I loved that. As I progressed through my career, I found it to be true over and over again.

CAMILLA

When I was a probation officer, I had a probationer, Camilla, who suffered from paranoia. Her symptoms could be kept under control with medication. The problem was that without Medicaid insurance, she could not purchase the medication necessary to maintain her mental health. Every time she went to apply for insurance, she'd get paranoid while sitting among strangers in the waiting area of whatever building she had gone to in order to apply for the insurance. She would act out; security would then be called, and Camilla was shown the door. And so the cycle continued: No meds. Paranoia. Acting out. Thrown out. Once, she was even detained by police.

Eventually, I got fed up with how the system was treating her. So I went with her to the application office, flashed my badge, and asked to speak to a supervisor. I explained the situation. "Look," I said, "when she doesn't have her medication, she gets agitated, which can escalate to violence. That's why she's on probation. I don't want anyone to get hurt just because she can't purchase the medication that she needs…do you? It's a simple solution to a difficult problem, and the resolution lies with you."

The supervisor looked over at Camilla who was still in her chair in the waiting room. She kept her head down to block out threatening stimuli.

"Listen, she needs to be seen right away," I continued. "I know it's not protocol to jump the line, but this isn't a normal situation. And you have the power to help someone who is suffering."

Again the supervisor hesitated. What did I need to do to break through the bureaucratic wall? Her name tag listed her full name, but I chose her first name to make the situation more personal:

"Norma…we really need your help."

Then, from the look on her face, I realized she was afraid to be alone with Camilla during the interview she needed to conduct with her.

"If it's all right with you and Camilla, I'd like to sit in on the interview," I said.

Camilla nodded, still not looking up.

"Okay," the supervisor finally said. "My office is back here."

The supervisor was a nice person, but during the interview, as a result of her efficiency, or maybe her fear, she practically shouted questions at

Camilla, stirring up her agitation, and mine too. It wasn't the supervisor's fault, she was trained to get her job done and move on. Lots of people were waiting for help outside her door.

"May I?" I asked, putting my hand out for the papers that needed to be filled in. Being uncomfortable, the supervisor handed me the papers then sat back at her desk.

I asked Camilla the questions. Sometimes, if Camilla hesitated, I spoke softer and more calmly, using a friendly voice. I don't know how the supervisor felt about my hijacking the interview, but she seemed interested in my approach.

Finally, all questions answered, I thanked Norma, and Camilla and I left her office. No violence, no paranoia on display, her insurance card on the way. Indeed, Camilla obtained her medication and remained stable throughout the course of her probation.

LUIS

The worst instance of patient dismissal I ever witnessed almost cost Luis his life.

When I was the assistant head of the counseling department in the outpatient methadone clinic, I often ran interference when crises arose. Luis often showed up at the clinic with his wife and two young sons who adored him. He had a job as a grocery store manager and had shown no signs of drug use.

One day, I received a call that Luis was in the emergency room. He had regressed and had overdosed. I had no idea what triggered his regression, but I rushed to the ER to check on him. I usually took a nurse with me whenever a medical situation like Luis's arose, but no nurse was available that day, so I went on my own.

When I arrived at the ER, Luis was unconscious. He was hooked up to tubes and a breathing device. Seeing Luis in that state was shocking enough, but what I heard the doctor say to the nurses stunned me further.

"I know you're busy," the physician said, "so remember this guy is a drug addict and will probably OD again, so save your energy for the other patients."

Never did I think prejudice would extend so deeply as to give permission to someone to let someone else die.

"Excuse me, doctor," I said. "Luis is a patient at my methadone clinic, so here's how it's going to go. If you don't do everything, and I mean everything possible to save his life, I'll report you to anyone and everyone in charge of your medical license. In addition, I will bring his two little boys who worship him in here so you can look them in the eye and explain to them why their father, in your judgment, was not worth saving."

Everyone stared at me, not knowing what to say or do. Then, the godlike physician found his voice.

"You don't belong in the ER," he said.

"From what I've just heard, neither do you," I said. As I left, I turned back around and added, "You don't know me, but I always keep my promises."

Luis lived. I hoped his near-death experience would spur him to clean up his life.

CYNTHIA

When did someone actually bottom out and rise above the horrible affliction of being an addict—an affliction that consumed the user, that destroyed families, and that often resulted in the addict having a criminal record and sometimes suffering a premature death? Was it possible to actually leave all of that behind?

Every time I lost hope, not just hope in my patients but hope in my own personal life, I thought of Cynthia: a woman who taught me about survival, and overcoming devastation, and, most of all, about the most precious gift a parent could bestow upon a child.

*

In my early career, I did not have the academic or experience skill level of some of my colleagues. But I had acquired two powerful traits: a heart that had been crushed and then healed after my mother's death, and a psyche that had survived the trauma of Gordy's sexual assault.

Cynthia had lost everything to drug addiction: her home, her family, her friends, and her two children, who had been placed in foster care by child services. She lived on the streets, prostituting for drugs and food money.

One day during Cynthia's downward spiral, she was found lying in the street, having collapsed from an overdose. She was transported to a nearby hospital and recovered...only to start the cycle once again. And then she told me about the triggering event that finally pierced her denial and brought her to the clinic. "I saw a friend of mine, Kerry, lying in the street from an OD," she said. She stopped as tears welled up in her eyes. "Kerry was taken to the hospital, and she did make it."

I waited. She needed to tell the story at her own pace, not mine.

"When I looked at her lying in the gutter, all broken down and filthy, like something the garbage man would pick up and toss in a truck...I knew that was me. What if my kids had walked by and saw me looking like a piece of garbage? Forget how they would feel about me, how would they feel about themselves?"

"How would they feel?" I asked as she gathered more tissues in her palm.

"That I didn't love them enough. That I chose drugs over them."

"Is that how you feel about yourself? That you're not worth loving?"

"I guess so. I never told you this, but my mother was also an addict. It made me feel like shit."

"I guess the question is, how do you want to view yourself and how do you want your kids to view you?"

"I know. I know. I think I'm ready," she said. "I want a new life. One with hope."

"If you feel you might slip, see me before using. And you need to get away from those using drugs. They'll suck you right back in. Do you have others that can be a support system?"

"One of my old neighbors said she would help. She even said I could stay with her while getting myself together. And no, she's never used."

"Sounds great," I said. "Keep asking yourself this question: do I want my kids to see me as an addict who failed them, or as a strong woman who overcame great obstacles?"

Her children were her vulnerable area, the weakest point in her denial system. I had used the image of my mother looking down on me to pull me from the abyss. She had used her children.

Slowly Cynthia took steps pulling herself from the edge. She had gone back for her GED, then started courses at a community college. Her goal was to become a teacher. After she was clean for more than a full year, I wrote a letter to social services recommending she be permitted supervised visits with her children. She obtained a job as a teaching assistant; eventually, her children were returned to her.

One day she brought her ten-year-old son and eight-year-old daughter in to meet me.

They were neat and clean, and smiling. As we talked, I saw how proud they were of their mother's comeback. The family laughed and talked with ease. Both children wanted to go to college, as their mother had done. The girl was going to be a teacher, the boy mayor of the city. He already had my vote.

But when I stepped back, I realized that besides being a survivor, Cynthia had given her children a profound gift: a sense of self, an assurance of their own individual self-worth. Besides love, that is the most precious gift one can bestow upon a child.

Cynthia was an inspiration to me, and she raised the bar for me, as she did for herself. I now knew how far a human being could change, and I vowed never to give up on anyone, no matter how broken the individual seemed. A ray of light shines brightly in each of us; it was my job to uncover it, and help that person harness its power.

LAUGHTER IS LIFE'S COPING MECHANISM

As competent as I felt after working a few years at the drug detox hospital, a curve ball arrived when I least expected it. And on this occasion it was mortifying.

And so onto the most embarrassing moment of my life….

Besides playing games with the patients in the dayroom and talking to them in their rooms during my first job at the drug detox hospital, my colleagues and I also planned outdoor activities. A local park had given us a permit to use the softball field one day a week: we looked forward to getting outside and interacting in a normal public environment. Our permit was confined to a two-hour period, so it was important that we organize the patients quickly and get them out the door of the hospital.

Mark and I took turns checking out the field for illegal contraband: needles, tubes to tie off an arm to make a vein pop so drugs could be easily injected. We even checked for heroin stashed outside (unfortunately we had to check inside the hospital on occasion as well).

While Mark went on his scavenger hunt through the park, I gathered the patients, telling them to line up down a narrow hallway. The hall was adjacent to the main ward by a locked door that lead to the exterior hallway and the elevator. The men gathered in the narrow hallway, waiting for me to unlock the door. I'd done the drill many times before, so it was routine. But I had no sight line into the narrow hallway…so I had no idea that this time two patients had decided to sit on the floor, their backs against the wall, their legs extended out in front of them. In a rush, I turned the corner and fell across the laps of the two patients sitting in the hallway. My awkward flop would have been embarrassing enough, but my shoes flew off, my skirt flew up over my waist, and there I was lying across the laps of the two patients, my ass in the air, my panties on display for all to see. Everyone was silent, no one moved.

Rule Number One: no touching of patients by staff. And vice versa. Trust me, no one trains you for situations like this anywhere.

I thought to myself: *With no help, how do I get off of these guys?* I couldn't crawl off of them the way I'd flopped; but because I'd have to use the patients' legs as leverage, I wondered what might happen if I touched an area by mistake that I should never—*not ever*—touch?

So with no help, and the deadly silence continuing, I decided to roll sideways down their legs to their feet, until I hit the floor where I could hoist myself up. My plan worked. Then, with the little bit of dignity I had left, I smoothed my skirt down while the two patients who had caught my shoes handed them to me.

I had no idea what to say. *"Sorry boys, show's over?"* That didn't sound appropriate. So I said nothing, and we all went to the park. To the patients' credit, they never laughed or said anything to my face. What went on in the privacy of their rooms, I'll never know. But I'm certain silence was not maintained there.

I told my boss Patricia (the one with the potato salad dripping down her arms) what had happened. I could see that she wanted to laugh, but she held it together and eased me out of my embarrassing trauma. But at the next departmental meeting for the recreational staff, Patricia got up and announced:

"I heard that a staff member had inappropriate interactions with some patients…."

Who the hell would do that? I thought.

Then, she pointed to me.

"Would you please tell the staff what happened?"

All eyes turned to me. I was shocked and speechless to realize that Patricia would divulge what I had told her during a private meeting.

Then, as I looked around, I realized everyone already knew, and they burst out laughing. Apparently, my ungraceful demise had spread all around the hospital. And then the teasing began.

"Hey, what color undies are you wearing today?" someone asked. "Can I see, or is the show private, for patients only?"

"Do your panties have lace on the edges?" someone else chimed in.

"I'm having a party next week and I'm looking for a stripper. Are you in?"

Talk about hazing rituals! The teasing felt as though it went on forever, and not just from my department. But as I said before, you can't work in places like this without a sense of humor, especially about yourself.

SEX, DRUGS, UNFORSEEN ADVENTURES

The staff at the detox hospital were young, eager, intelligent, social, and a lovable group of oddballs. Someone once asked me what is a normal person?

"Boring," I answered.

I love people who can get out of their own skin, and this group had it all. That was one reason I didn't enjoy the temp office work I'd done before; everyone was so buttoned-up.

But after spending your day locked up in a pressure-cooker situation, helping other people, weekends were the time to break out. *Let's party!*

And party we did. We had lots—and I mean *lots*—of parties. I think fun, laughter, spontaneity became the salve to our sometimes traumatizing work week. And here's the insane part. We were working with drug addicts—and what did we do at our own parties? Yup, we used drugs. Not heroin, but pot. And hash smoked in large, sculptured water pipes. And uppers. *And* downers. *And* LSD. *And* lines of cocaine.

The walls of our parties rippled with laughter, teasing, everyone high on one drug or another. Some partiers—the ones still dressed in buttoned-up work clothes for the weekend shift—looked hilarious in their outfits while inhaling marijuana and bouncing off the walls, high as hot air balloons.

It was that infamous era of sex, drugs, and…well you know. We indulged in it all.

Here's the other crazy part: we all went back to work completely sober on Monday, ready to do our jobs. One can't work in places like the detox hospital when not fully alert. No hangovers allowed. As years went by and our adult responsibilities increased, we stopped using drugs altogether.

So why didn't we all become addicts? I've thought about that whenever I heard that pot is a "gateway drug." *Any* addiction can be a gateway drug: alcohol, gambling, sex. All these stimulants are readily available to the public, and if used or enjoyed in excess will ruin anyone's life.

I've seen individuals with gambling addictions lose jobs, their families, their children, wind up in jail, and deal with shady dangerous individuals who are not fun to be around, especially if you owe them money.

So why don't we ban all of the above? We tried that—right?—with prohibition. Didn't work, did it? Whatever is banned finds a thriving home in the underground. And because it's illegal, addicted individuals don't seek help.

Those who engage in their drug of choice will sometimes get addicted, others will not. Some control it, others don't. Why? I've seen people snort heroin once in a while and not get addicted. Once someone moves on to shooting up on a regular basis, they're finished. But I've seen others' skin pop on occasion, and they never become an addict.

Is it body chemistry? Is there an addictive personality? Was the drug used for fun or as a means to deal with personal problems? Some people, like Cynthia (the addict who had overdosed) clean up. Others keep regressing over and over and over again.

I know I don't have an addictive personality, so I never worried about my behavior at the parties. I never took pills or used LSD, which frightened me. I did do pot, hash, and lines of cocaine. But once I left the party, that was it until the next party, which might be a month or two away.

Most of us were young, vibrant, tasting every aspect of life. Mark was dating a woman named Lainey who worked on the all-female unit of the detox hospital. I started dating Steve, a medical supply sales rep, and the four of us often went to movies, theater, concerts, dinner together. We were good friends who had formed a makeshift family.

Steve was a real sweetheart, kind, caring, fun. My first non-Jewish boyfriend. Sometime after we moved in together, I went home with him to the mid-west to meet his parents. They embraced me as one of their own.... Was a wedding in our future?

Around that time, women's lib had taken hold; our coworker, Laurie, attended a consciousness-raising group. Participants in the group got together to discuss their lives, their kids, their husbands, their hopes, their dreams, their disasters including domestic violence, which was rampant in those days.

If you were a victim of abuse and called the cops, they'd come to your door and ask you:

"What made your husband hit you?"

"I got home late," the women would say, "and didn't have dinner ready on time for him."

The cops' response? "Well, don't do it again and you'll be fine."

And then they left.

Here is a true story. A woman from Laurie's consciousness-raising group had recently had a baby. For some reason that fact made her husband more violent; the woman became worried about the safety of the child. She knew she would not receive the proper help from the police. So some of the women in the group went over to her house in the middle of the night, raised a ladder up to her window, and helped her and the baby down to the ground.

A car drove up and took the woman and baby to a safe house where other women dealing with similar situations resided.

As was the case for other safe houses, the location of the safe house where Laurie's colleague had gone was secret, as the police and the women's husbands were continually searching for them. Because Laurie's colleague had fled to a safe house, she necessarily was cutting herself off from anyone she ever knew. She was also starting over again with a bunch of strangers in a new environment. What a pathetic situation! Luckily, Lainey and I never encountered violence in our relationships.

*

Laurie, Lainey, and I used to have lunch together at least once a week. You know, girl talk: the type of emotional exchange—a sharing of intimacies—that often makes men flee the room. But we loved it.

Lainey and I were curious about all the details of Laurie's consciousness-raising group. When she told us a lesbian was in her group, we looked at her in surprise. *"What?"*

Neither I nor Lainey had ever met a lesbian, at least not that we were aware of. Everyone, and I mean everyone, was in the closet back then....The local media had covered the story of two women who had been seen near the Hudson River piers, kissing passionately and holding hands: they had then been viciously raped and beaten by a group of men. Even straight women were harassed back then. If you passed a group of men, especially men who were working on a construction site, they made lewd comments and grabbed their crotches, letting us know how manly, how sexually alive they were.

That's what it felt like back then: women as objects of male sexual aggression, male violence at home. In the street there was very little support or acknowledgment from the powers that be, who were of course all men. No wonder women's lib came into being. Enough, as they say, is enough. Women are not particularly prone to violence; instead of fists, we formed groups and talked and supported each other. And we marched.

*

Lainey and I decided to join one of the consciousness-raising groups. It turned out to be an eye-opener in more ways than one.

I didn't realize how much discrimination women suffered until it was lain right in front of me. Lower pay, sexual touching at work, rapes, harassment, domestic violence—all occurring with no voice and little support from the community.

At the group Lainey and I attended, I also met my first "out" lesbian. I'd been heterosexual my whole life, so I was fascinated with her story. Was a lesbian born this way? Did it evolve slowly? Was it genetic?

The consciousness-raising groups were safe spaces for sharing and caring, not overthrowing the government. No violence whatsoever. So how come an FBI undercover agent was planted in our consciousness-raising group?

That's right, we thought she was one of us, a married woman with children, a stay-at-home mom. That was the story she gave us. She joined our group for a few months, then her "husband" got a job out of town and she and her "family" moved to another state. Then, while I was watching the news one night, who shows up on the TV with a gun at her side, a badge around her neck, walking a handcuffed perp into a police vehicle? Yup, our stay-at-home mom. Did the FBI really think a bunch of women sitting around sharing their lives would blow up the city? Was the feminism movement that terrifying to the government that they had to plant a spy in our midst? The sole purpose of groups like ours was to talk freely and safely.

Lainey, Laurie, and I had lunch that week. Laurie had been living with a man named Seth for at least a year at that point. So when she told us that she was having an affair with a woman from her consciousness-raising group, we almost fainted.

What? Hello? How the hell did this happen? Lainey and I were stunned by the news; we couldn't stop talking about it. Woman-on-woman, what the heck was that like?

Lainey and I were as close as best friends usually are, and with Steve and Mark we had a fine little group, a lot like a family. But I couldn't get the notion of this woman-to-woman thing out of my mind. What would it feel like? How could two women actually have sex together? What did they do?

Lainey was very adventurous, and I was always curious to learn more, so one day we went to a sex shop in the Village. There were all kinds of—what shall I say?—*accoutrements* available for sale: whips, chains, leather masks and outfits, dildos of every size, shape and color, outfits for role-playing, books on various sexual activities, and videos for watching in the privacy of one's own home.

Here I am, my self-image that of a tough girl from Brooklyn, blushing as I made my way down the aisles. I had never seen anything like these things before, nor did I know these particular items existed, nor what they were used for.

Lainey was brave enough to buy a vibrator: we rushed to her apartment to figure out how the damn thing worked. We laughed our heads off as we turned it on and the thing took on a life of its own. We placed it near our crotches, vibrated, and got hysterical again. Neither of us was about to put one of those things up our vaginas. We had numerous questions:

"How can this be sanitary…?"

"Can it rip open my vaginal canal….?"

We made up scenarios of unusual things we could do with the dildo. We thought of not telling Steve or Mark about our purchase, putting it in the bed between us, and then, when we were making love, suddenly turn it on and watch them freak out. We laughed so hard and felt so high on this new experience we had to smoke a joint to calm down.

The next week, Lainey and I went to the movies together as usual. I have no idea what picture we saw as I could not concentrate on the screen. I don't know what happened, I really don't, but all of a sudden, I became aware of Lainey in a new way, a very potent sexual way. All I wanted to do was put my hand on her thigh and touch her in a show of intimacy. Of course I didn't. But as we continued our normal routines, coffee shops, movies, consciousness-raising group, double dating with Steve and Mark, my sexual feelings grew more and more urgent. It got to a point that the need to be physically intimate with her became so uncomfortable, I didn't know if I could sustain our friendship.

I started observing how she walked, the movement and swing of her hips, the smell of her shampoo, the way her eyes lit up two seconds before a belly laugh erupted.

I knew others thought she was very attractive, but I'd never paid attention to that. I had been drawn in by her intelligence, her sense of humor, her social daring, her compassion for others, and my total trust in her when sharing intimate thoughts, feelings, and emotionally vulnerable parts of my life.

My time with Lainey became frightening and confusing.

I hoped my feelings were just curiosity and would pass over time. But they didn't, they only deepened.

Here I am living with Steve, a lovely man who'd taken me home to meet his parents. What did my feelings for Lainey say about my love for Steve? Was it just Lainey I had feelings for, or would I be attracted to other women? Had something hidden been awakened in me? Was I straight, gay, bisexual?

I didn't know who I was anymore. The confusion tightened like a noose around my neck. I became more distant from Lainey and Steve.

I knew I couldn't talk to anyone at work about my confusion. How about a therapist? What if she was straight, would she understand my dilemma? If my feelings came out in public would I still be able to work at my job? And what about Mark, my work partner, who was Lainey's boyfriend? And of course Steve?

Times were *so* repressive back then. Once during a team meeting with other counselors in a different hospital, a female counselor began discussing a treatment plan for one of the patients she had been working with for over a year. We all suspected the counselor was a lesbian—but like I mentioned earlier, *no one* came out back then. The counselor excused herself from the team meeting early, as she had another appointment to go to. After she left, the rest of us weighed in on her treatment plan. All of us agreed it was a good one and on target.

Then, the head psychiatrist who was leading the meeting said, "Well, what does she know? She's a lesbian."

What does she know? I thought. *What do you know? You never even met the patient!*

The silence in the room after the head psychiatrist's pronouncement was stunning. Although we all respected the counselor and liked her as well, no one said a word to defend her. No one. Not even me.

Coming out was dangerous back then on many levels. A woman could have her child taken away from her as an unfit mother. She could lose her job, with her administration department giving some lame excuse. She could be beaten or gangraped like those women holding hands I mentioned earlier. She could be ostracized by friends, family, and colleagues.

It was a perilous time for me to even *think* about being with Lainey. It would ruin both of our lives.

EMERGENCE

I continued to hang out with Lainey, but I was constantly on my guard not to show any inappropriate feelings toward her, not to let any words slip out of my mouth that might clue her into the attachment and attraction I felt for her.

One day Lainey invited me over to see something she said was special. Her living room windows faced the windows of another building. Apparently, she had neighbors across the way who liked to leave their blinds up when they were engaging in sexual activities.

So of course, I wasn't going to miss this. It was like the Alfred Hitchcock movie *Rear Window*. The erotic neighbors must have wanted others to observe their actions…some special thrill they shared knowing an audience was watching them. Their acrobatics were so carefully choreographed, we felt as if we were watching a stage performance from the balcony seats.

Lainey and I laughed, cheered (even though the couple couldn't hear us), smoked a joint, then sat stoned on the couch next to each other.

I don't know why, maybe because I was stoned and relaxed, or maybe my ability to filter my thoughts was turned off, or maybe I just couldn't hold my impulses in check anymore, but I decided to bring up my "elephant in the room." I mentioned Laurie's affair with the woman from her consciousness group, which, by the way, no one knew about except for Lainey and I. Laurie knew we would never have violated her trust.

"Did you ever kiss a woman?" I asked.

"No, did you?"

"No," I said. "Did you ever have a crush on a woman?"

"Occasionally," she said.

"How did you handle it?"

"I didn't."

I guess that was my answer: she didn't. Now what?

I looked at her and smiled, she looked back at me and smiled. Then suddenly, I don't know how it happened, I wish I could explain it, but we were kissing. Not a peck on the lips. But a deep, down-in-your-soul kind of kiss.

When our lips unlocked, we looked at each other. I jumped up and ran to the other side of the room. We were both mortified. What did we just do?

"I guess we shouldn't have done that," I said.

"I guess not."

And so I got my jacket and left.

I did not see Lainey that week as she worked on a different floor, and I was grateful that we didn't run into each other. But I was still working with Lainey's boyfriend Mark every day. I don't think he picked up on anything odd during my interactions with him, as he was excited about his upcoming trip to see his relatives in California. That was all he talked about.

I managed to keep everything together around Steve. As a medical equipment salesman, he was often on the road. I was glad that week when he left on a business trip. I needed time to think and process what had happened between Lainey and me. If we moved forward with the relationship, it would devastate both Mark and Steve…Perhaps we would lose our jobs if it got around, or we'd be alienated from our friends and family members. I was in agony. I had no one to talk to and no one to ask for advice.

All I knew was, I'd never felt the depth of emotion and experienced the psychological intimacy I was experiencing now. I'd never experienced it with *anyone*—not even with Donny, my first love.

I had a nice life. Was it all going to blow up on me because of one kiss? I ruminated for days, and then I called Lainey.

"Hello," she answered.

"It's me."

Dead silence. I waited. Then I said:

"Do you not want to talk to me?"

"Actually, I was hoping you'd call."

"You were?"

"I miss you. I want to be with you."

The sigh of relief I expelled had the force of hurricane winds.

"Believe me. I want to be with you so badly, but—"

"I know. I know," she said.

"Do you think we're sick?"

"I have no idea. I just want to be with you."

Her response was more than I had hoped for.

As Steve was away on business, and as Mark was visiting relatives, we made plans for Lainey to come over to my apartment on Friday night. She arrived with an overnight change of clothes and some pajamas—and never used any of it. We literally stayed in bed the entire weekend…naked. We showered together, called for take-out meals in our bathrobes, then shucked the robes and went back to bed. And, unlike her neighbors across the way from her apartment window, we kept the blinds down.

I had never felt such elation in my life. We were cocooned in this false reality of momentary safety, exploring each other's bodies slowly and carefully, asking permission before touching certain areas, then checking in to make sure all was well and enjoyable. The talk, the touching, the giggling constituted a masterclass in female lovemaking.

At one point I had so many orgasms, deep, continuous ones, that I was afraid I would break my clitoris. I found out that part of my anatomy was *very* resilient. The entire experience felt beyond the boundary of my physical being. And that included not just the physical aspect, but the emotional and psychological aspects as well. Maybe some of it was due to our hormones, but the rest was pure joy.

But then the weekend was over. Steve was due back on Tuesday, Mark later in the week. We called in sick on Monday. The guys returned, and we went back to our normal routines. No one suspected anything.

Lainey and I had very little contact at work. At our weekly lunch with Laurie, we mainly listened to her regale us with her stories of the week. But we never shared our story with her.

I basically lived a double life. I had it worse than Lainey. She only had to lie and pretend all was well with Mark. I had Steve at home, then Mark at work to deal with. I felt guilty, confused…but most of all high on Lainey. I'd never experienced a heroin high, but in a way, I imagined the high I felt with Laurie was more potent, because there was no coming down from the drug. It was a constant elation, 24x7.

We needed to see each other, but how? Neither Steve nor Mark was going away anytime soon. So we started to invent extra consciousness-raising group sessions and events; but instead of attending the fake events, we went to motels in the area, paid for a full night, then stayed a few hours, making love, talking, becoming more attached to one another. Time was needed to see if we could sustain a relationship. We decided to take a trip down south, a part of the country neither of us had ever visited before. A "girls" trip.

How was the trip? I have no idea. We traveled through multiple southern states, but spent the entire time in motel rooms. When we went outside to eat, we bought postcards to send home and souvenirs to bring back to the guys to support our "girls trip" lie.

Soon enough the stress was getting to both of us. The lying, the cheating, the guilt, became unbearable; after a while, Lainey felt that Mark suspected she was having an affair. He was right, but not about who his rival might be. And I was covering for her on a daily basis, giving Mark our fictional excuses. The tension between Mark and Lainey increased at home.

Had Lainey withdrawn from him further after our "girls trip?" Whatever it was, Mark moved out, and there I was at work, soothing him over his broken relationship—and I was the one to blame. Who or what had I turned into? I'd never wanted to hurt anyone, especially Mark, who I now cared for deeply. Yet, I was the cause of his pain.

Lainey kept assuring me it was her choice to be with me. And now that her apartment was free, she hoped we could finally live together. But what about Steve? He was clueless that anything was going on behind his back. Mark's pain was bad enough, but now Steve? Kind, sweet, loving Steve! He had upended his life and moved out of his previous apartment, setting himself up in a larger one, so he and I could be together. Whenever he looked at me, nothing but love shone in his eyes.

Steve went out of town frequently, and I ended up staying at Lainey's apartment while he was gone. Lainey's place began to feel like home to me… The compatibility and ease of our relationship blossomed further and further.

Lainey never pressured me to move in with her, even though she told me how much she would love it. But the decision was mine. I envisioned our wonderful life together until I couldn't stand it anymore. I had to tell Steve.

But what should I say? That I turned into a lesbian over night? No one could know that. The consequences would be monumental.

I know it's hard for those growing up today to understand how dangerous, on many levels, coming out at that time could be. The fear of being ostracized, losing employment on some phony pretext, becoming alienated from family and friends, and the great violence that might be committed against us…these were all real and very palpable risks.

How should I tell Steve? Should I start picking fights with him until he broke up with me? I was already doing a bad enough acting job leading two lives, how would I pull that off? What was I doing? Who was I?

If I stayed with Steve, I knew he would always love me, be attentive to my needs. We would have a sweet, calm, normal life. Being with Lainey meant jumping off a cliff and falling into an abyss with no idea where I might land.

I decided to make the leap.

*

"I've fallen out of love with you," I told Steve after sitting him down one day.

"What? What does that mean?"

What the hell *did* that mean? How does one fall out of love when there are no issues? When all has been as lovely as it has always been?

"What did I do?" Steve continued. "Tell me, please. I'll fix it. I don't want to lose you."

My heart ached with guilt, the pain I was causing him.

"Is there someone else?"

How could I tell him I'd fallen in love with a woman—especially our dear friend Lainey.

"It's just that I feel differently. I don't know why."

"I don't understand."

Of course not. I didn't understand either.

"I thought you loved me. I brought you home to meet my parents. If you need more time…"

"Your parents are lovely people," I told him. "It's just…I don't know. Something changed inside me and I can't commit to the relationship."

"I don't want to pressure you, so take your time. Just know, I'm here for you."

You know the shock people experience when there's a blow to the head and they can't process anything for a few minutes? That was the look on Steve's face. Only this time the blow was to his heart. He said nothing, just breathed heavily. Then tears slowly crept down his cheeks.

I'd never seen him cry before. All I wanted to do was comfort him, tell him all would be okay; but that would have added another lie to my growing list of duplicity.

I kept repeating over and over again how sorry I was. But what kind of apology makes amends for ripping someone's heart apart?

And I knew that look in his eyes oh so well. The total abandonment, the looming loneliness, the grief over loss. I knew the faster I moved out, the faster he would heal. At least that's what I told myself. Was that just my selfish rationale to soothe my own conscience?

I moved into Lainey's, Steve helping me pack. Can you imagine that? Steve helping me pack. What a sweetheart! When we hugged goodbye, I don't know what I said, I just knew it would never be good enough to mitigate his pain.

I kept in touch with Steve for a while, but life with Lainey became all-consuming. We were constantly involved in one activity or another. I was the more conservative stay-at-home type, but I went on all of the new adventures with her. I would have followed her anywhere. She introduced me to ballet, modern dance, country music, classical music, art, architecture, and New York history.

While we were out exploring and having fun, Steve often left drunken voice messages for me at Lainey's apartment. He hardly ever drank while we were together.

"I love you…I want to be with you." He pleaded with me to come back.

The calls became a regular event. After a while, I didn't know what to say to him anymore. I stopped answering his calls, hoping he would move on. Eventually, he moved back to his hometown, and the calls stopped. I hope more than anything that Steve found the love of his life and has everything he ever hoped for.

THE DOUBLE LIFE

Throughout this period, Lainey kept me grounded. She knew how to calm me down and alleviate my guilt. I grew more and more attached to her. My love and lust for her grew stronger and stronger every day. We had a need to break out of our "roommate" undercover mode and have some fun. But how?

Around this time, our consciousness-raising group heard about a lesbian bar. Well, not exactly a bar. You've probably heard of the Stonewall Inn, which was indeed a bar—a *full* bar—for gay men. It was there for them full-time. But back then the only venue expressly available to lesbians for socializing was a bar in a restaurant that hosted a "woman's" night once a week. That was it.

I'll call the restaurant bar Rosie's.

The bouncer at Rosie's would stand at the door and tell heterosexuals who might have eaten there during the week that a private party was in progress, and he could not let them in. Then when a woman or two women or more showed up, they had to give the bouncer a password. Yes, a password, like in the old speakeasy bars during prohibition. After all, what was more prohibitive than a woman loving another woman?

Well, Alcoholics Anonymous had their password, "I'm a friend of Bill's." We had Dorothy.

I was never exactly sure how the password for Rosie's came about; I was told it was based on the character of Dorothy from *The Wizard of Oz*. In those days, the drag queens loved to imitate Judy Garland singing "Over the Rainbow," and they were incredible. But how did "Dorothy" become the lesbian password at Rosie's? Maybe because she dreamed of going over the rainbow to a better place? I guess that was the dream all of us lesbians dreamt. But for now, we only had Rosie's Bar and Restaurant on Wednesday night.

Neither Lainey nor I had ever been to a lesbian event, probably because there weren't any. At least none that we knew of. Nor did we know any of the lesbians outside the consciousness-raising group. We were completely isolated in our double life. But the minute we told the bouncer at Rosie's "Hi, I'm a friend of Dorothy's" and actually stepped inside Rosie's, a surge of elation overwhelmed us.

The place was packed with women, all dancing in a totally uninhibited way. And drinking. And laughing. And making out in corners. *Wow! Wow! And wow!* I almost cried at the sight. We were no longer alone.

We immediately ran out onto the dance floor, and I went wild. I *love* to dance…to fling my body every which way. Lainey, in this setting, became more conservative, but she bobbed and weaved quietly to keep me company. I can't count how many people I danced with that night. Everyone danced with everybody. Women danced alone on the dance floor, they danced in groups, all of it totally spontaneous, totally free, totally nonjudgmental….It was as if we all had burst out of jail, at least for one night, and we were going to get high inhaling every moment of it!

And whose idea was it to present woman's night every Wednesday night at Rosie's?

Wait for it….

The Mafia. At least that was the rumor.

Yes, that devout Catholic religious group might be hosting lesbian night at Rosie's bar, and whatever their value system was at home, *this* was business—and a cash business at that. No one was catering to the lesbian crowd; they knew a great opportunity when they saw one. And we were all grateful.

Until that night, I never knew how many lesbians were out there, isolated like us. All of us were desperate to meet other women like ourselves, to have fun in a safe environment: no violence, no rape, no harassment, no identities outed to others. Whatever your perception is of the Mafia, at that moment, dancing at Rosie's bar on a Wednesday night, they became our saviors. They treated us like royalty and kept us safe inside. When we left the restaurant the door person always looked back and forth down the street, making sure no one was lurking about; then he signaled us when his surveillance was complete. He kept an eye on us until we were out of view. Words could not express our appreciation.

*

Things back at the detox hospital began to heat up. I don't know whether Lainey and I had started giving off some kind of vibe or whether the fact that we had left the guys and moved in together had led our coworkers to start gossiping, but our colleagues began to suspect the truth. We were more than friends.

Some seemed suspicious—their attitudes bordered on malicious. Others, such as Laurie, our lunch mate, were thrilled to believe it might be true.

We left Laurie to her fantasies and never confirmed or denied anything.

The worst situation was Mark, who pretty much guessed what was going on.

The tension at work continued ramping up. I didn't know how much longer we could stay there.

Lainey, the brave, daring, adventurous one, suggested we quit our jobs, leave New York, and head across the country.

Huh? Where would we go? What would we do? What about earning a living?

After my mother died, I craved safety and security. But, I craved Lainey even more. I couldn't believe I was agreeing to the madness, but in truth, I would have gotten on a rocket ship to Venus if it meant I could be with her.

So, we sold our furniture, sent anything we wanted to keep to her mother's house in St. Louis. We bought a car, and that was it. We were ready for a hippie adventure. We sadly said goodbye to friends, had one last dance at Rosie's, and took off for parts unknown.

Just as Black travelers to the South had a list of places to stay where they could feel safe (as fictionalized in the movie *Green Book*), the lesbians of that day had a list of places where they, too, could stay while feeling safe. There were also lists of Rosie-type bars where lesbians could hang out with other lesbians. Unfortunately, when we tried one of the establishments from the list, we discovered it was located underneath a train track trestle in a dark, deserted part of town….This was supposed to be a safe place? Maybe it was safe inside, but who was lurking outside?

I admit, never having been outside of New York, I found it was fun roaming the country with no schedule, no real purpose. We blasted the car radio as we passed farms, cornfields, never seeing another human being; then we moved on to big cities and crowded populations. We even met a group of friendly wanderers who were sharing a meal in the parking lot of a motel. They invited us to join them. We did—and we had a great time.

*

I met real cowboys in the West, bull wranglers who went from town to town, traveling the rodeo circuit. They'd say "Howdy, Ma'am." That was the first time I'd ever been referred to as "Ma'am." I'm not kidding.

They were a delightful group…One of them asked me out for "a burger." Unfortunately we had to leave; but I would have loved having a burger with him while being regaled with stories of being a real cowboy. They all had fabulous tales to tell about their time on the rodeo circuit, all of the broken bones and injuries they'd sustained trying to tame unruly bulls. I felt bad for them.

More sightseeing followed until reality took over. Little money, no jobs, no home.

We headed back to New York.

The two "roommates" rented an apartment in Manhattan. How Lainey and I managed to pass a credit check, I don't know, but we did. Then we had to look for work.

Based not only on her previous experience working with the women in the detox hospital but also on her work in the psychiatric unit, Lainey found a job at a psychiatric hospital. On the first day on her new job, the hospital's elevator door opened—and out popped Laurie, our lunch friend from the detox hospital. And guess what? She was now a lesbian too. She had broken up with Seth and paired with Sandra.

Was there something in the water—or perhaps the air-conditioning system—at the detox hospital? Or did the freedom the feminist movement gave us allow us to explore our internal selves, awaken parts of ourselves we had no idea existed?

Whatever the reason, Lainey and I immediately had new friends. Laurie, Sandra, and the two of us immediately became a foursome. We had dinners together, shared holidays together.…and with our return, we made the welcome discovery that a couple of full-time lesbian bars and restaurants had opened up.

Things had changed. But it still was not safe to be out at work, or with family. And it certainly wasn't safe to hold hands on the street. So our double lives continued, albeit with a few more outlets for freedom than before.

Soon it was time for me to get back to work. I decided to take the civil service exam to become a probation officer. Why? I had really enjoyed working with the male patients at the detox hospital, and many of them were involved in the criminal justice system. For some reason, I was always fascinated by trials and court proceedings.

As I worked on a practice test for the exam, a startling revelation emerged. Lainey was the first to spot it. I have what I think is a peculiar form of dyslexia. I had always done well in school and on standardized. The only two subjects I had a problem with were typing in junior high school and geometry in high school. But it wasn't math per se that I struggled with; I had aced trigonometry and algebra. My dyslexia had something to do with shapes and pictures.

Together, Lainey and I read the instructions for the practice exams. But when Lainey had finished reading the page, I was only halfway through. After talking with Lainey, I realized I did not read in the way fully-abled readers do. Most readers scan the words on the page, but I have to "speak" each word individually out loud in my head, or else I do not retain what I am reading.

When I took standardized tests for reading comprehension in high school, I finished at the same time as everyone else, so I had no clue that I read any differently from my classmates. Looking back, I think whereas my classmates had to reread the first paragraph whenever there was a multiple choice question about it, I did not have to go back and reread the story, because the details had stayed in my mind as a result of my speaking the words out loud in my brain.

I had no idea that I did not read like most people.

Visual shapes eluded me, however; that's why the keyboard and the three-dimensional shapes of geometry caused me problems. My father once did a math teacher's taxes for free, in exchange for the teacher tutoring me in geometry. I just about passed. In junior high, I had high marks in all subjects except typing. I had to stare at the keyboard, recognize each letter, and then type it. Everyone else's fingers flew across the keyboard like they were a piano virtuoso! Because I did so well in the rest of my subjects, I guess the staff thought it would be ridiculous to hold me back for being a slow typist. They passed me with the minimal grade for the course.

On top of that, I found out I had a facial recognition problem. Not with people I knew well, but with people I had met, let's say, at a party or several times at different events. We'd have nice conversations…but if I ran into them a month later on the street, I couldn't remember who they were. They would come over to say hello, and I had to wait for some clue in the conversation to trigger my memory.

My friends are all aware of this problem. If we go to a party and there are people whom I've met several times before, they will subtly clue me in to the person's identity. (Thank you, friends, for saving me from embarrassment!)

So many times, difficult events in my personal life helped me relate to other people experiencing their own difficult situations.

MARCUS

Marcus, an outpatient in the methadone clinic, walked into my office and asked me to help him fill out an employment application for a job stocking supermarket shelves. I scanned the form, it seemed fairly simple: name, address, prior employment history, and an essay about why the applicant wanted to work at that particular market. No big deal. I figured Marcus wanted help with the essay portion. I handed him a pen.

"Okay," I said, "fill in your name, address, and prior employment, and I'll help you with the essay."

Instead of taking the pen, Marcus looked away. He then glanced at the newspaper on the corner of my desk. I looked at the headlines but saw nothing unusual. Suddenly it dawned on me. I handed him the newspaper.

"Please read the headline for me."

Marcus closed his eyes, his head slumped to his chest.

"You can't read, can you?"

He shook his head, shame wafting off him. How had he gone through life unable to read? I never knew how crippling illiteracy could be until Marcus shared his story.

Marcus was literally confined to the neighborhood in which landmarks helped him traverse the streets. Outside those boundaries, he was lost. He could not navigate the subway or bus routes, as he could not read names of streets or the stops on train stations. He led a double life, hiding his secret from others, diverting their attention from his difficulty through humor or, sometimes, aggression.

By now I knew well about leading a double life, hiding secrets from others. And I was also well aware of reading difficulties, having finally recognized my own. Fortunately for me, my reading issues did not impact my life the way it did Marcus's.

"You know what I love about your problem?" I said.

Marcus looked at me like I was nuts.

"It's totally fixable," I said. "I wish all problems in life were this easy to solve."

I told him about places where adults like himself learned to read, no judgment, no pressure. He reacted ambivalently, but I convinced him to try it.

By the time I left my job at the clinic, Marcus was reading at grade school level. As I said, I wish all problems had readily available solutions. But passing my civil service test, and becoming a probation officer had its own set of challenges.

BREAKING THE BARRIERS

I was about to start my new job as a probation officer, but I knew breaking down the barriers between myself and my probationers would be a more difficult challenge than my work at the detox hospital.

At the hospital, me, my coworkers, and patients were all locked inside the unit together. I was able to play games with the patients, speak to them privately in their rooms, allow them to see me in a more natural setting. The need to connect with other people is a basic human function and under the less intimidating circumstances of the detox hospital, I was able to connect.

As a probation officer, I worked behind a desk, or interviewed suspects and convicted criminals in a jail in a lockdown area. I had the ability to send someone back to court on a violation of their probation, or recommend prison in a pre-sentence investigation report. In many ways, I was an authority figure. I'd taken the job to help others, but how could I establish trust and a working relationship under these circumstances?

To add to the barriers I encountered, my office was located in the court building where many suspects had been convicted and some of the other probation officers roamed the hallways while sporting guns on their hips and badges around their necks.

Even under normal circumstances, probation officers must overcome numerous external barriers in order to create a working relationship with their probationers: different races, different religions, different education levels, different economic classes. The list goes on and on. But on the internal level, we all had commonalities: the need to be seen for who we were, to be validated, accepted, cared about, and understood.

One of my patients at the detox hospital once asked me, "How can you help me? I'm a gay man. You know nothing about my life." Did that mean the only person I could help had to be my twin—a gay man helps a gay man, female helps female? What about age? Who sees an eighty-five-year-old woman who recently lost her husband of fifty years? Most people are retired by that point. And what about a terminally ill person? Do we have to resurrect someone from the dead to help out? If we did "twin" client to counselor, wouldn't that client lose the opportunity to learn about other life perspectives and skills different from those in his or her community?

I thought back to my days at the detox hospital. How had I been able to help other people so different from myself while also gaining their trust? First of all, I learned how to listen. Not the kind of listening where I told myself to keep quiet, wait until my patient was finished talking, and then say my piece. No. The kind where I had to do my best to see inside you and your situation and what you were feeling in your world. Then, if I didn't understand something, I asked questions, and I didn't get defensive if I was confronted with my own ignorance. It was a chance for me to learn from other people.

There is no better trait than authenticity. That, perhaps, is the most important thing to remember. On a subconscious level, other people realize that you genuinely do care, and they are willing to take a chance and trust you. Patience is a virtue in these settings. Acting out, challenging me at times is part of the process of being tested by clients. Being nonreactive, waiting and listening—*really* listening—is the antidote. It's not always perfect, but it does provide a jumping off point where you can at least get started.

Once the bond between us is formed, the experience of working together is enriching on both sides of the relationship.

There are two main aspects to the job of being a probation officer. One part of the job is performing pre-sentence investigations, the other is supervising probationers in the community. When I first became a probation officer, I started off doing pre-sentence investigations, which are reports given to the judges prior to their pronouncement of their sentence, but after the individual in question has already been convicted either by plea deal or trial. The reports were detailed and involved. I had to go to the district attorney's office and obtain the details of the individual's crime; then I tried to interview the crime victim (if he or she was willing to speak to me) to obtain a victim statement. The reports also included a list of prior arrests and convictions (if any); a section on the individual's social history in regard to his or her family situation, education, and work history; mitigating and aggravating circumstances; and a recommendation as to probation or prison. An example of a person whose suspected crime might have mitigating circumstances would include a mentally ill homeless person who was starving on the streets and stole food from a market but hurt no one. Aggravating circumstances might include an assault of a clerk by the same homeless man as he robbed the same store, even though the clerk did not resist and readily handed over the money.

My first case involved a complicated financial embezzlement committed by an accountant at a real estate investment company. I had enough trouble learning how to read—and now I had to untangle an interlocking web of debits, credits, false and real inventories? Of course, why not!

I was a wreck. Yes, I'd done many "intake" interviews before, but this was different. *Far* different. The stakes were high. What if I did not "read" a person properly and as a result put a violent individual back on the street who later went on to hurt someone else? What if I was overly harsh with someone who was basically a decent person, and who under a particularly harsh set of life circumstances committed a crime he or she would never again commit, but who, with help, would become a decent citizen of the community? Although the court would make the ultimate judgment regarding the person's fate, how I wrote the report, the areas I emphasized, the tone of my report, my recommendation regarding jail time or probation, could influence a person's freedom and future. I did not take my job lightly.

As anxious as I was conducting my first interview, the convicted embezzler I interviewed was even more of a wreck. He was sweating like a pig. I didn't know which of us would have a nervous breakdown first.

My supervisor was smart. He had set me up in the office where I conducted that first interview, and he sat in the office next to me to listen in on the interview over the half wall between us. I started the interview. As I talked with the embezzler, every once in a while my phone would ring. I answered it, only to hear my supervisor on the other end: he helped me, suggesting questions to ask and things to say to the person in front of me.

The embezzler had gotten himself into trouble by living a lifestyle beyond his means. And so he cooked the books and embezzled funds. He had no prior criminal history and had lost his marriage over the situation. He did have a bachelor's degree, and genuinely seemed like a decent person. He had been offered a job from a friend as an inventory clerk in a car parts business, where he would not have access to any of the company's financial books.

After concluding the pre-sentence investigation and consulting with my supervisor, I recommended supervised probation for the embezzler. I also recommended he pay restitution to the company from which he had embezzled the funds. His fear of jail was so potent, I believed the prospect of being imprisoned would serve as a legitimate deterrent against further criminal activity. In addition, in the case of a white-collar crime such as embezzlement, the victim often desires restitution, which cannot be accomplished unless the embezzler is either very rich (which our embezzler wasn't) or employed.

*

Individuals who had been arrested for a crime, but who were not released on bail and who necessitated a pre-sentence investigation were brought into a holding prison area monitored by corrections officers. That's where I met my next convicted felon: a violent mugger who had assaulted a woman on the street, taken her possessions, and beaten her pretty badly.

The interview area was located in a secure part of the building. To get there, I had to take an elevator run by corrections officer then walk down a hallway to the interview space, which was surrounded by prison bars. Inside stood a few rows of desks with partitions between them. The probation officer sat on one side of the desk, the prisoner on the other side.

All of the probation officers inside the interview room seemed relaxed. I had already met most of them by that point, so I felt perfectly comfortable in the confined area. A corrections officer was posted at the entrance of the interview area and opened the gate to let us in and out. A second corrections officer escorted the prisoners back and forth between the interview area and their holding cells, until they were eventually transported back to the formal prison by bus.

The prisoners understood that the stakes were high. They were controlled and respectful, and they probably had been oriented by their lawyers about what was considered proper behavior to exhibit during the interview.

When I met my first prisoner, all seemed routine. I joined the other probation officers at my assigned table, where I began my interview. I was alone in the interview area with my prisoner. I did not think anything of it, until something unexpected took place: the CO, who assessed that my interview was going smoothly, locked the gate and left his post. I was now locked inside the interview area, no way out, with a man who had brutally beat a woman.

So there I am talking to this guy, getting the information I need, and all of a sudden, this weird look of scrutiny comes across his face, like a thought bubble had turned on somewhere inside his brain. He leaned forward menacingly and stared into my eyes from across the desk. Then he said:

"It was you, wasn't it?"

Huh? I thought. *What the hell is he talking about?*

"You turned me in, didn't you?"

Uh oh. I remembered the district attorney's report had mentioned that a female witness had witnessed the crime and testified to the brutality of the defendant's actions. But it sure as hell wasn't me. Now what?

Was he faking mental illness? His essence told me no. He had already been convicted in court, and his defense lawyer would have used mental illness as a mitigating factor, but did not.

The prisoner was now breathing heavily, becoming agitated, daggers shooting from his eyes. I realized it would be best just to end the interview, but there was no corrections officer to let me out. I needed to buy time. I remembered what the shrink at the detox hospital had taught me: if a patient gets agitated or starts hallucinating, ask him about something concrete that he has to think about. So I took a chance.

"What did you eat for breakfast this morning?"

As off-the-wall as this question sounds, I knew I had to shift the prisoner's attention onto something concrete; hopefully it also showed my concern for him. He stopped talking, confused, unable to process the sudden change in topic and tone.

"Are you getting enough food?" I asked again.

"Yes," he said hesitantly.

"What did they give you to eat?"

"Huh? Is this important?" he asked.

"Yes, it is. It's part of the interview process."

He looked away from me, trying to regain his equilibrium.

"Oh, okay."

After he relayed the details of his morning meal to me, we went on to dinner the night before. I was running out of food questions while trying to figure out my next best strategy. Finally, the corrections officer returned. Thank God! I stood up.

"Well, it was nice meeting you, and I wish you well."

I smiled lamely at the corrections officer as I left. I said nothing about how he had endangered me, nor did I report him. I'd already been schooled by my colleagues about prison culture: reporting an officer could result in a dangerous situation for me during another interview, when I might be abandoned to deal with the crisis on my own.

Eventually, I shifted from only pre-sentence investigations to supervision of individuals who had been convicted and sentenced to probation. The supervision lasted anywhere from three years to five years depending upon the severity of the crime. It was counselling-oriented and more to my liking.

The probationers had to adhere to all provisions of their sentence, such as paying restitution, holding a full-time job, staying away from certain people. Each case was different. I had the option to visit the person at home or work, as I saw fit. If the individual missed an appointment or violated the terms of probation, I could request a warrant to bring the person back to court on a violation of probation.

I enjoyed the work, made new friends among my colleagues, and became familiar with court officers, corrections officers, and administrative staff all whom worked in different areas in the same court building. I felt totally safe everywhere I went in the building.

So how did I become a crime victim while I was in the middle of a building filled with trained law enforcement officers and some of my colleagues armed to the teeth? Did it happen in the passenger elevator?

Nope. How about the downstairs lobby? Nope. Then the surrounding sidewalks outside? Nope.

The crime took place right in my supervisor's office.

Now that I was supervising probationers, I had weekly sessions with my supervisor to review all aspects of my caseload. My supervisor was a well-respected, dignified man, a church elder. He was quiet-spoken, with a graceful bearing, and always formally dressed.

One Friday morning, I went to his office, sat in my usual wheelie chair at the side of his desk, and began the update of my probationers' lives, and any interventions I'd made that week to help them get back on their feet. As I was relaying my notes, all of a sudden, from out of nowhere, my supervisor leans forward, puts one hand on each arm of my chair and wheels my chair toward him. Then he puts one hand behind my head, forcing my face in his direction, and sticks his tongue down my mouth, reaching all the way down to the place where my tonsils used to be before I had them removed. *Hello?* What the hell was going on here?

Why didn't I stop him? I had no idea what he was doing until it was too late. I was totally stunned. I couldn't think straight. I guess I could have bitten his tongue off, but this big slimy blob owned me at the moment. I couldn't move. I couldn't do anything. I was literally in shock. Finally, he pulled the offensive attacker out of my mouth, leaned back, and smiled at me.

It was not a lascivious smile, but more like a soft, "wasn't that a lovely interaction we just had?" smile.

No, it wasn't. It was disgusting.

Now what? I wondered. Do we go on as if nothing happened? Will the slime creature come out at me again? What do I do?

As his gentle smile stared at me, I shoved my feet forward to gain traction and wheeled myself to the door. I opened it and sped down the hallway on my own private chair-scooter, turning the corner toward my office as my colleagues laughed, thinking I was playing a prank.

Once I had reached my office, I left my private scooter outside the door, went inside, and collapsed in my chair. Thank God my officemate, Cece, was there.

"What's going on?" she asked.

"You're not going to believe this," and I related my story.

"You gotta be kidding," she said.

"I wish I was."

Cece was as shocked as I was, and she stood up to return my chair scooter to my supervisor's office. Turned out he wasn't there. He was probably off molesting someone else, or perhaps masturbating in the men's room.

Cece and I talked and talked about the best way to handle the situation, but we agreed that no one would believe my tale. Here was a man who'd worked in the probation department for decades, was in his sixties, dignified, well-respected, no complaint against him that we knew about. What chance would I have to make my charge stick? What proof? What credibility had I earned being new to the job?

So we agreed that I couldn't say anything as the blowback would be directed at me. If I'd ever had a learning experience as to why survivors of sexual assaults at their workplace stay silent, it was then.

There was no "Me Too" movement back then. And Cece and I agreed that when I went to my supervisor's office the next week, I would leave the door open, and Cece would come by on and off, looking in, waving at me, so my supervisor would know he was being watched. He said nothing, I said nothing, about the incident. We simply continued our working relationship.

About two years later, rumors started to swirl about my supervisor's behavior during a field visit to a young, female probationer. When I heard this, my first thought was: *Why is he making a field visit?* He was a supervisor. The probation officers made the visits, not the supervisors. Next I heard he was taking early retirement. By that time, I was integrated enough into the office to be in on all of the gossip. The word was that my supervisor had made inappropriate sexual advances toward the female probationer, and the young woman's mother had reported him.

He retired with a full pension, suffering no consequences.

Later, I'm in one of the stalls in the ladies room, and I overhear two women who are standing at the sink while discussing my former supervisor.

"He did it to me," one of the women said.

"Me too," the second one said.

I flew out of the stall, half dressed, yelling:

"Me too!"

There apparently were five "me too" women in the office. None of us had reported the supervisor for all of the same reasons. Each of us had determined that no one would ever believe us, and our reputations would suffer irreparable harm.

Shortly after this incident, I was sitting around with four friends while relating my story to them. I was astounded to hear that each one of them had been through similar events, some much worse than mine, perpetrated on them in their workplace. None of us knew about each other's incidents, none of us ever talked to anyone about it back then. We all lived in silence, feeling guilt, maybe shame, just as I had felt after Gordy's sexual assault on me as a kid.

Gratefully, female victims of sexual assault no longer need to be shrouded in silence, nor remain underground in a secret society. Please, speak up. There are now other women who will support you.

THE PAST OOZES INTO
THE PRESENT

Sometimes the past catches up to us in profound ways. We live through the good, we live through the bad, never knowing how our past will affect our future.

SHERRY

Sherry was a convicted felon serving five years on probation. She had robbed a drug store, stealing certain prescription drugs, and taken money from the register; but she hurt no one during the robbery. But why a drugstore with cameras and security when she could have gotten most of the drugs on the black market?

Her explanation: her boyfriend at the time needed medication for kidney problems. She robbed the pharmacy to make sure the drugs were of high quality rather than buying them off the street, where you never knew exactly what was inside the pills. Apparently, the boyfriend's insurance would not pay for the prescription drug he needed. Sounded plausible, but something didn't feel right. What, I didn't know. It's crazy how one can develop a sixth sense when working in a chaotic and volatile environment.

Sherry came to my office hostile and immediately shut down, her bitter rage permeating even "Hello." She answered my questions as minimally as possible, and she did not discuss details about the crime beyond what was already written in the pre-sentence investigation. Apparently, she and the boyfriend had since broken up.

"How is your boyfriend doing?" I asked.

"I don't want to talk about it," she replied curtly.

She lived with her sister's family, worked at a hair salon, and brought her paycheck stubs to me each week. No matter what I said, I couldn't break through the wall of anger. Her passionate loathing for me was palpable.

I had a good relationship with most of my probationers and was able to lend them my support. I provided advice and referrals to other agencies as needed. But not with Sherry.

All went well for the first two years. I accepted that I was not going to break through her wall of hostility, and my responsibility for Sherry, at least on paper, was successful: no subsequent arrests, she remained fully employed, and she kept showing up for her appointments with me. Then, her pattern changed.

Sherry began missing appointments, always calling with a plausible excuse: she had to work overtime, or a family member was sick. But then she would show up for her next appointment acting as naturally as before. Something didn't add up.

I contemplated visiting Sherry's workplace, where supposedly the other workers were aware of her probation status, so my appearance would not have been a surprise. Then, I received a call from Sherry's sister.

"Sherry's in the hospital," the sister told me, "so she can't make her appointment today."

"What happened?" I asked.

"She collapsed in the living room yesterday."

What was going on? Was she using drugs? I hardly knew her.

"Collapsed?" I asked.

"Yes, the cancer finally caught up to her. She's dying."

Cancer? Death? *What?* I thanked her sister for calling, took down the hospital information, and called to verify that Sherry had indeed been admitted. The hospital of course would not give out medical information, but I had her room number.

How could I not know that she was seriously ill? I should have picked up on some clue, but no, nothing. Was she so great at the cover-up, or was I blinded by her hostility and not paying proper attention?

What do I do now? I wondered? Do I go see her and offer support? How would she interpret my showing up in her hospital room? Would her dislike for me make my visit more harmful than helpful?

Truth is, I felt like a failure. How could I have allowed so many impenetrable barriers to be created between us—barriers that meant I knew nothing about her life-and-death struggle? I solicited advice from a few friends in the mental health field, friends whom I could trust. All of them encouraged me to go see Sherry.

I decided I would visit her on a Sunday, during my off hours, and dress down, not in my professional clothing, just informal weekend wear, hoping my appearance would help lower the barriers between us. But that's not what happened.

When I arrived at the hospital, Sherry was asleep, no other visitors were in the room, her roommate's bed was empty. I sat patiently waiting for her to awaken, the IVs pulsing fluids into her body, the monitors beeping. The familiar smell of the body rotting from inside out brought back the horrors of my mother's last days on Earth. I hadn't expected my reaction—then suddenly Sherry opened her eyes. I had to hold my own feelings in check. I was here for her, not my past.

She looked around, at first disoriented to her surroundings, then her sight shifted in my direction. It took a minute, but then she recognized me.

"What the hell are you doing here?"

"I came to visit," I said. "Your sister called me and—"

"Well, you can take your ass and march it out the door."

She turned to face the window. With nothing to lose, she could talk to me in any manner she chose.

"I'm sorry about what you're going through. I just thought—"

"What, that you'd check up on me, make sure I'm really dying, not just skipping out on our appointments?" she said. "Huh? Is that it? Well, don't worry, you won't have to see my sorry ass ever again."

And with that, the tears streaked down her face.

I handed her a box of tissues. She took one, but did not look at me.

"Thanks for dropping by," she said. "You can go now. Your job is done."

With that, she turned away from me again. Why was I there? To assuage my sense of failure or to provide some comfort to her? But how?

We sat in silence for a while. I took the fact that she didn't tell me to leave again as a good sign.

"You know," I said. "I've been through a situation like this with a family member."

"Oh yeah, when?"

She turned her face back toward me, challenging my assertion, but I saw a slight glimmer of curiosity emanating through her glare.

"My mother, when I was a kid."

Normally, I would never talk to patients about my personal life, but this was not a normal situation. I relayed parts of my story to her, parts that she could relate to about the hospital, the treatments, the doctors, the nurses never mentioning the "terminally ill" part. She listened intently, shook her head in an empathic way, especially during the part about me being a kid. And then the dam broke.

Sherry talked of her symptoms, the treatments, the doctors she liked, the ones she hated. Then, she related how her former boyfriend, who had set her up to steal the pharmaceutical drugs, turned out to be an addict, not a kidney patient. How everyone in her life, except her sister, had failed her. I nodded here and there, letting her spew forth all of her past misery, her guilt in disappointing her parents and some of her friends who eventually abandoned her.

Here she was, basically alone except for her sister and me, a stranger sitting a few feet away. I listened with compassion, no judgments, occasionally only a supportive response. This was not a therapy session. Looking back, I see it as more confessional on her part, taking stock of her life, relieving her guilt, perhaps in some way asking for forgiveness.

At that point, I understood the need people have for a member of their clergy to be present at the end of their lives. A neutral party who listens without judgment, but unlike a priest, I had no prayers of absolution for Sherry, just a desire to listen and help ease her burdens.

When Sherry started to breath heavily and then became silent, I knew it was time to leave.

As I stood up, she smiled at me and extended her hand. I took it and held on until she let go. Then, I left. That was the last time I saw Sherry.

*

Trying to ease Sherry, reliving the nightmare of my mother's death, was bad enough. But after two years at the probation department, the bottom dropped out again.

The city was in a severe financial crisis, and civil servants were being laid off. The plan: last hired, first furloughed. Guess which group I was in?

BACK TO BASICS

At home, Lainey and I loved our life now that we were back in the city. So much to see, so much to do.

Along with our newfound lesbian friends Laurie and Sandra, the hub of our social life became our centrally located apartment. Straight, gay, men and women, most from the psychiatric hospital where Lainey worked: all came together for meals, to hang out, to gossip about the hospital. They embraced us as a couple without prejudice. But I did not feel that same comfort level on my job at the probation office. I did make some friends with whom I could be myself, but the wild spontaneity I had enjoyed at the detox hospital was a different vibe than the rules and regulations of the court system.

Being furloughed from my probation job was a blow to my sense of self—and to Lainey and my financial security. Lainey and I pored over our budget and decided that given her salary and my unemployment checks, I could afford to go to graduate school for social work. No jobs were available at the time; even though I went through the motions of job hunting, I had to bide my time until the economy improved. Going to graduate school might make me more employable and maybe allow me to earn a higher salary in the future, if I was not rehired by probation quickly enough.

And so I applied to a graduate school program in social work that fast-tracked students who had already been working in the field. Classes were held at night and field work was conducted during the day under approved supervision.

One of our new friends from the psychiatric hospital where Lainey and Laurie worked became a part of our social group. But unlike the others who worked on a traditional psych unit, Joanna worked on the all-male psychiatric prison unit within the hospital. She and I became best friends for life. When I was laid off, I talked to her about her unit and wondered if I could do my field work there.

What better way to combine my mental health skills with my criminal justice experience? If you've ever felt you belonged in a certain community, this was mine. As Joanna said many times: "You either have a calling for this type of work, or you don't."

But the hospital's all-male psychiatric prison ward was not on the school's approved list of places for field placement. I'm not even sure how many people knew the place existed. The three counselors on the unit were all men, but their supervisor, who did not have an office on the unit, was a woman. Apparently, there had never been a woman social worker on the all-male unit. So I wasn't sure my asking to do my field work there would fly. Maybe because I dared to ask, maybe because of my experience in the court system and in a drug treatment program, both the social work supervisor of the unit and the head psychiatrist agreed to allow me to do my field work there. I still needed approval from the school; my advisor scheduled a visit to view the unit.

As far as I knew, nobody had done field work inside a psychiatric prison before. What a great learning experience it would be! But then I hit a snag. To understand what happened next you need to know the layout of the unit.

Access to the unit was through a steel door that only a corrections officer could unlock. The steel door led to a small hallway with bars on either side. Basically, until the corrections officer opened one set of bars or the other, leading to two separate housing areas, one on the right, one on the left, anyone such as myself was trapped in a small hallway. Nearby stood a locker room where patients exchanged their clothing for hospital garb.

One side of the unit opened into a larger hallway where staff offices and the nursing station were housed. Past the offices, behind another set of bars was the men's sleeping area, eating space, and TV day room.

When my school advisor came to the unit to assess it for my field work, she was let into the small hallway. I immediately saw a look of horror on her face. Her eyes darted every which way. I literally thought she might faint. After the tour, we went to the hospital cafeteria to talk.

"How can you work here? There are bars on your office windows."

"I know," I said. "It's a prison." I didn't mean to be disrespectful, but of course there were bars.

"Don't you feel claustrophobic and unsafe?"

"No, the corrections officers will protect me, and the office is about the same size as other places where I've worked. There is plenty of light despite the bars on the window."

"I don't know. I don't know," she said.

What was going on with her? Was she going to deny me a phenomenal chance to learn new skills while working amid a population I was already familiar with?

"You know," I said, "we're taught to provide services to all people. These men may be locked up, but they're still humans. Isn't that the value system we're taught in school?"

I really liked my advisor; I liked her so much. I had learned a lot from her, and I respected her. But I'd never seen the side of her she was showing me now.

"Please, tell me your objection to my working here besides the bars on the window, which don't bother me in the least," I said.

Anyone in the field of social work who holds a position of authority, at one time or another has to decide when or if to reveal personal information. I hoped my advisor would take the leap. She did—and I was not expecting to hear what she told me. She vividly related a tale from her youth. Her country of origin was in the midst of a civil war. She and her family had to flee after nightfall to the safety of a bunker below ground level: no light, no outside air, no time frame regarding when or if they would ever be freed. Her imprisonment lasted for weeks. She occasionally heard gunfire from above. Obviously, she and her family did escape and arrived safely in America. But walking onto the prison unit, locked in the small hallway, bars all around, triggered a flashback of my advisor's childhood fear and trauma.

"I did not want you to go through what I had as a child," she said with a bit of embarrassment. "If you're sure you want to work here, then okay."

As I argue throughout this book, you never really know someone until they're willing to share their deepest thoughts and feelings. I thanked my advisor for her honesty, and I checked in with her at school from time to time, just to let her know I was fine.

*

I wasn't sure what type of outfit I should wear for my first day at work on the prison unit. Joanna gave me certain instructions. First: no sexually suggestive clothing, nothing high-end, just regular clothes. Second: no dangling earrings or necklaces, scarfs, or anything a patient could grab and use to strangle me. Third: nothing on my desk that could be thrown and turned into a weapon. Oh, and yes, flat shoes in case something went down and I had to run for my life. Who wouldn't want a job like that?

My first day on the prison ward was overloaded with stimulation. So many moving parts: different staff functions, procedures, priorities—and loads of patients.

Even though the prisoners were in a prison environment, they were considered patients as they hadn't been convicted of a crime, only arrested. Our job was to evaluate anyone perceived to be mentally ill at the time of arrest. The criteria was whether the individual was mentally competent enough to participate with a lawyer in his own defense; the criteria was not whether the individual was guilty of the alleged crime.

If a patient was evaluated as being mentally stable, then he was arraigned. If not, we provided short-term treatment consisting of one month of counseling, psychiatric testing, and medication. If the patient responded, he was released from our ward and deemed ready for arraignment by the court. If his illness was not responsive to our methods, he was sent to a longer term inpatient facility for treatment. He was then returned to us a few months later for reevaluation to determine whether he was now able to understand the procedures and work alongside his lawyer. Besides administering treatment, part of our job was to separate the fakers (malingerers) from the genuinely ill patients. Those trying to fake illness were looking to present mental illness as a mitigating factor. This was especially true in murder cases.

Patients were with us for a month. It is very difficult to feign mental illness when under twenty-four observation by dozens of staff members from different disciplines. How many people can keep up a charade of that magnitude when half the time they don't even realize they are being observed? Not only doctors but nurses, counselors, corrections officers, and activity therapists were all part of the team.

I shared the social work office with three men. I thought they might resent having their space invaded by a woman, but they were friendly, supportive, funny, and committed to showing me the ropes.

The psychiatrists and the psychologist, who performed psychiatric testing, went out of their way not only to teach me, but to invite me to sit in on interviews with highly unusual cases. Experiences I had on this unit were invaluable, and could never have been taught by a textbook or a lecture. All the knowledge and skills training I received had to be gained not only through observation but through living and feeling experiences firsthand.

And then there were the nurses, who were headed by Mrs. Mays. Mrs. Mays was a toughie, the proverbial bull in a china shop. Nobody messed with Mrs. Mays. I mean *nobody*. She scared the hell out of me.

I saw Mrs. Mays in action one day with a difficult patient. Finally fed up by his behavior, Mrs. Mays walked over to the gate behind which were the patient quarters. She stood on her side of the bars and called out in a loud, deep, booming voice:

"Wilson! Wilson! Get your ass over here now."

All the staff froze in place. Wilson, knowing he was in trouble, shuffled meekly to the gate.

"Yes, Mrs. Mays?" he asked in a tentative voice.

Suddenly, Mrs. Mays whipped her hand out from behind her back and presented Wilson with a hypodermic needle that could kill an elephant. I'd never seen such a long, thick supposedly medicinal rod in my life. Was it real or a prop from a horror movie? She held it at Wilson's eye level.

"You see this, Wilson? Well, do you?"

"Yes, Mrs. Mays," Wilson whimpered. "I hear one more word about you acting out, just one more word, I'm gonna come in there and shove this needle so far up your ass it'll see daylight at the other end. You got that Wilson?"

"Yes, Mrs. Mays."

"Now get your ass back to your bed, and shut the fuck up!"

Wow! I'd never encountered that type of therapy before! I watched Wilson hightail it back to his bed. So yes, Mrs. Mays was tough, but as I learned over time, she was also very sweet, kind, and compassionate.

When I first arrived on the unit, she called me into her office. This was before I had witnessed the Wilson episode, and I was already freaked out by her. But in her office she was warm and smiling and asked me a few questions about myself. I warmed up to her. Then she said, "Look, this is not an easy place to work. Sometimes it's chaotic and scary. But you seem competent and I'm sure you'll get the hang of it."

"Thank you, Mrs. Mays," I said, grateful for her support.

"Now, anyone gives you any trouble, you come to me, and I'll make sure it never happens again, okay?"

"That's great, thank you."

After what I had witnessed with the elephantine hypodermic needle, I had no doubt about the veracity of her statement. She ran a tight ship, but the staff respected her for that.

*

One day, a patient became seriously ill. An ambulance was on the way to take him to the emergency arm of the hospital. I watched as Mrs. Mays sat by the patient's bedside, holding his hand and reassuring him that all would be okay. She did not leave his side until the transport arrived.

I wish the corrections officers had welcomed me with the same care as Mrs. Mays. But instead I was greeted with hostility and a subtle form of harassment. Each time I called "On the gate" to be let into one part of the unit or another, I was made to stand in that small hallway near the unit's entrance for several minutes until the gate was unlocked. It was a subtle form of harassment; I wasn't sure why it was occurring. At first I thought it was because I was the only female social worker working there. But the nurses were not harassed, nor was Joanna, who worked as an activity therapist on the unit. I didn't understand why I was being harassed, and I wasn't comfortable seeking anyone's opinion or advice because if my query got around the unit it might cause me to be further harassed. So I smiled and waited and acted as if nothing unusual was happening.

After I'd been on the unit for several months, an incident occurred that changed my relationship with the corrections officers, and with myself as well.

A prisoner at a local jail had violently and severely attacked a corrections officer. I happened to be near the steel door entrance waiting for a patient to be brought to me for counseling, when the violent offender who had attacked the corrections officer was escorted onto the unit. He was handcuffed and accompanied by two corrections officers. The prisoner then was led to the locker area where patients changed into hospital clothing and were searched for weapons.

All of a sudden, I heard the steel reverberation of someone being slammed into the doors of the lockers. Then, moans and groans as fists, kicks, and slaps were administered to the newcomer's body. Then, he was escorted from the locker room into the housing area, his face swollen, his leg limping.

The corrections officer on duty by the gate stared at me, a severe warning delivered through his eyes. Joanna had told me about a male therapist who had reported an abusive guard to the administration. When a patient went berserk and attacked that therapist, the guards turned their backs and were nowhere to be found. The other patients pulled the attacker off the staff member.

What do I do now? I thought. I had always sworn I would do everything within my power to keep my integrity intact until the day I died. If I ratted out the corrections officer I would be in danger whenever I was on the unit. If I kept quiet, I would lose my self-respect. I knew within prison culture payback for hurting a guard was commonplace: either the offending person would be abused by other corrections officers or another prisoner would sometimes be set up to deliver the abuse to the perpetrator in exchange for favors at a later date. And so I pondered my options. My deliberations were brought to a halt the next morning.

Once again I was near the entrance to the unit when a man of obvious authority entered the unit; he was followed by two other men. The first man turned out to be the warden. I stood perfectly still, not understanding why the warden was here. The corrections officer who had given me the stare down warning the day before was on duty again. He deferentially greeted the warden, who then turned toward me.

"I heard there was an incident yesterday when a prisoner was brought in from another facility, and that he then needed medical attention. Were you here at that time?"

I wish I could have disappeared into oblivion. I hesitated then said, "Yes, I was."

I could feel the corrections officer stare slice through me like a razor blade.

"Did you see or hear anything unusual at the time?"

This was the moment I dreaded. Of course I had to be the one standing there, near the entrance to the unit, when the warden came in. I had no chance to gather my thoughts. I stalled as long as I could. The warden waited. I think he understood my quandary.

"No, sir, nothing unusual happened," I said meekly.

He nodded and continued to the locker room. The corrections officer gave me a subtle smile. No, let me correct that: he gave me a smirk. I canceled my appointment with my next patient, left the unit, and went to the cafeteria, appalled at my cowardice. I rationalized my choice by reminding myself that the offending prisoner was getting a beating by someone at some point, no matter what. You don't attack a corrections officer and expect not to suffer any consequences. Was it worth endangering myself by trying to stop the inevitable? I wish I could have discussed it with Lainey, but I didn't want her to worry about me at work. So I stayed isolated in my dilemma.

The next day, something peculiar happened. I went to the gate and asked to see a patient. This time, I was not made to wait in the small hallway. The patient was brought to me right away, and a corrections officer was assigned to stand outside my door and protect me as I interviewed the individual. I'd never had a protection detail before. I understood this was my thank you gift.

What surprised me the most was that my lapse in integrity turned out to be a bonus for one of my patients: Wendell.

WENDELL

Wendell was the last-born in a family of twenty-one children who lived and worked on a farm down south. Wendell had allegedly murdered someone. (Remember, no one is guilty until proven so in court, or until they take a plea deal.) I don't remember the specifics of the alleged murder, but then neither did Wendell. That fact was often stated to us on the unit. Either our patients claimed they blacked out at the time of the crime, or else were too drunk to remember why they were arrested. Were these statements true, or were they excuses?

Whatever the reason, my job was to evaluate the individual's ability to participate in his own defense, not to decide guilt or innocence.

Wendell was tall and slim, but he was muscular as well, an imposing presence if not for his shyness.

He behaved like a little boy trying to please his parents. This behavior was in opposition to what the corrections officer had told me. Wendell was difficult to deal with, and he didn't respond to orders. I couldn't reconcile the little boy in front of me with the defiant adult the corrections officer complained about.

Wendell had no prior record, he was cooperative. But I did notice something a little off in our interviews. Anyone else would have been highly anxious in the interview situation, but Wendell's anxiety level was beyond the usual. He was like a sentry on patrol in a hot zone.

I asked him about the complaints from the corrections officers. He kept apologizing, saying he would do better, but the complaints kept coming.

As I was waiting near the patient TV room one day, I saw Wendell watching a program with the other men. The program they were watching was a comedy: the room would erupt with laughter at a physically funny bit or a hilarious line of dialogue. Wendell had no idea that I was nearby, and as I observed him, I noticed something peculiar. Wendell laughed a few seconds later than the rest of the men in the room. He was watching them then mimicking their responses. Suddenly, after putting all of the pieces together, I had a hunch about the underlying issue. I went to the psychologist who was working the unit and asked him to test Wendell's IQ.

Sure enough my hunch was correct. Wendell had a low IQ. He could not process speech or behavior patterns as quickly as others, and multisyllabic words were difficult for him.

I went to the corrections officer, who was now my "friend," and called in my favor. I explained the situation and argued that when Wendell was acting disorderly he was not, in fact, being disobedient, and I asked if the corrections officer could share the information with the other corrections officer. Perhaps they could speak more slowly and use simple language when giving Wendell orders? They did as I suggested, and suddenly Wendell became less anxious and was no longer seen as a problem patient.

Did the treatment I received for Wendell assuage my guilt over not ratting out the corrections officers who beat the prisoner in the locker room? Some days yes; other days, no. But I never would have been able to help Wendell if I hadn't made that choice, or so I told myself.

FLYING SAUCERS AND
TIN MEN, OH MY!

Because I was on the prison unit to learn as part of my credit for my clinical degree, the head psychiatrist often invited me to sit in on unusual cases. I was able to see a man who was certain aliens had infected his brain, schizophrenics in the midst of psychosis, individuals with suicidal depression, and on and on—mental health issues one would read about in a textbook, in a theoretical, intellectual way, but never experience in person.

One day when the psychiatrist invited me to sit in on an interview, I processed that something was askew as soon as I sat down. Perhaps the doctor was distracted, I don't know, but he broke a cardinal rule: never leave anything on a desk that can be turned into a weapon. Volatile patients, plus creative weapons, spelled trouble.

The patient was brought in. He sat opposite us, on the other side of the desk. I couldn't concentrate on the interview, as I kept glancing at the phone sitting on the desk. Sometimes, subjecting a patient to a stressful interview can blow their cover of feigned mental illness, as the agitation of coming up with answers in real time often causes them to revert back to their true selves.

I felt the stress building as the doctor pushed on. I saw the patient glance quickly at the phone, and I made the instantaneous decision to duck under the desk. The flying phone was hurled so fast and so forcefully that the doctor probably prevented himself from getting a concussion by leaning to his left side. As soon as the phone hit the back wall, the corrections officer subdued the patient and led him away.

The doctor, who was still shaking, apologized to me. I assured him it was okay, but it wasn't. He had been careless and endangered both of us. I did not accept another interview "sit in" from him.

ROBERTO

The experiences I had on the prison ward remain, to this day, unlike any other situations I've confronted on any other job. For instance: Roberto. He entered my office with stiff legs, almost as if marching in a band. I greeted him and asked his name.

"Roberto…robot."

Are you kidding? That's the best you could come up with?

"Well, Roberto, please have a seat."

The act of sitting turned into a major event as "Roberto" did not know how to fold his "robotic" legs in order to sit down. I had to hold the chair for him, so he could bend his legs at the knee and basically fall onto the seat. Unfortunately for him, at the end of the interview, he had forgotten he was mechanical and stood up easily. He finally remembered to lock his legs on the way out. By then, it was too late. The ruse had been unveiled.

SYLVIO

My first interview with a schizophrenic patient in the midst of psychosis literally left me speechless. The police often brought the patients from the street straight into the unit, no medication, no assessment. Everything Sylvio said to me made sense in that the sentences were correctly put together, but the thought process were so scattered and rapid that when we were done, I couldn't put my own logical thoughts together afterward. It scared me. I asked the psychiatrist about my scrambled brain.

"You've just seen your first patient in the midst of psychosis," he said. "If your brain is fried afterward, use it as a diagnostic tool to confirm your diagnosis."

Thanks a lot. I was now a nervous wreck, worried that my brain would be forever impaired.

After being medicated, Sylvio eventually returned to a semblance of normalcy. And somehow so did I. It was astounding to see how intelligent and thoughtful Sylvio was when not in the throes of psychosis. I realized what a nightmare it must be to possess no control over your thought processes. And that was another lesson for me: stay with the patients in their reality. Trying to talk them out of it only increased their agitation.

*

From my experiences at the detox hospital, the probation department, and the psychiatric prison ward, I found I had a new-found ability to quickly size up a situation, juggle through possible interventions, and act with confidence to make an intervention. These skills translated into my everyday life.

HEROIC? NAH!
JUST ME BEING ME

Why do some people run into danger and others do not? This puzzle has been studied for years. Do some individuals have a more evolved primitive survival instinct that is constantly on high alert for danger?

Perhaps because of my heightened sense of awareness that came from dealing with bullies as a child, or perhaps because my mother was suddenly taken from me, or because I worked in volatile environments, I developed a sense of environmental awareness and a feeling of responsibility to jump into unsafe spaces.

The events I'm about to reveal will sound unreal and maybe make me look like a lunatic—especially if you recall how small I am. But I assure you, they all took place.

One day, as I was about to cross a four-lane street (two lanes in each direction), I heard a commotion across the street. A crowd had gathered around a man and a woman who were fighting. The man was slapping, kicking, and punching the woman, who was completely helpless to defend herself. She was screaming, "Help me! Please, help me! He's gonna kill me!"

Obviously, the woman was genuinely in distress, and her assailant was hurting her badly; he was totally out of control. Perhaps more astonishing was the fact that the crowd stood around gawking as if at a sporting event. No one intervened even though there were several large men in the viewing audience who could have taken the man down. Some at least yelled "Leave her alone!" and "Let her go!"

Others…dead silence. I quickly calculated my odds against the large, violent man, and I realized I could come up from behind him without drawing his attention. So that's what I did. Then I leaped onto his back, wrapping my legs around his waist to gain some support; then I placed my hands over his eyes and pulled his head backwards.

"Men, where are you?" I shouted, over and over again to wake them from their stupor. I didn't know how much longer I could hold on.

Finally they woke up and took action, wrestling the perpetrator to the ground. Of course, he landed right on top of me, breaking my glasses. But the woman had been saved. The cops were called, and I slid away. I had done my job, now let everyone else stay and give their statement.

Another time, I saw a bike messenger wearing a backpack run over an elderly man, who dropped to the ground. I did not want the biker to get away, so I ran across the street, grabbed the biker by his backpack, and threw him off the bike. Then, I shouted, "You may not leave the scene of an accident!"

The messenger was so shocked, looking down at me, that he froze. Luckily, a cop was nearby and put him against the wall. I then gathered the gawkers and had them form a circle around the victim, who was bleeding from his head, to protect him from oncoming traffic.

"Don't move him. He may have a spinal injury," I said.

I assigned a woman to call an ambulance, which she did, and it arrived quickly, taking the injured man to a nearby hospital. Afterwards, that same woman came up to me and said, "You were very brave. How did you do that?"

Another time I was sitting on the subway late at night after leaving a party. I picked up that the guy across from me, a few seats away, was observing me. I guess I looked like an easy target sitting down. I secretly watched him as everyone left the train car. He and I were the only ones left. I wasn't certain of his intentions so I waited until the train pulled into my stop. Then as the doors were closing, I jumped off the train. He was able at the last minute to block the door and jump off after me. We were alone on the platform. I wasn't going to be a passive victim.

I turned and walked toward him with the most out-of-control look on my face that I could muster. Then I started screaming at him.

"You fucking bastard! You think you're going to attack me?" I put my hand in my pocket as if I had a weapon. "Go ahead, asshole, just try it!"

I stared at him for a full minute unmoving. He looked flustered—and those few seconds of doubt allowed me to run upstairs and out of the subway. I checked behind me to make sure he wasn't following me, and then I went home. Was he going to attack me? I don't know but I wasn't going to take a chance. If he wasn't, he must have thought I was a total nut job. Who cares? I've been called worse.

When I was in college, I was riding the train with some friends, and we were sitting side by side studying for exams. All of a sudden, this guy stands right in front of me, opens his coat, and spreads out the sides like the wings of a swan. I looked up. He was exposing himself, giving me and my friends on either side a private view of what he must have thought was his greatest asset. I whispered to the friend on my right, "Don't look up now, but there's a penis staring at you."

Of course there's no greater motivation to look up than a phrase like that. As his erection grew like Pinocchio's nose, I decided to teach the man a lesson that hopefully he'd never forget. I spread my book out all the way across my lap, and as the train pulled into the station, with all the hustle and commotion distracting him, I slowly raised the opened book then with all my might slammed it closed on his infringing member, leaving him screaming at a pitch even opera divas could never duplicate. Then, as my friends and I called him "pervert" and "loser," we laughed our way off the train. I wonder whether he went to the ER and how that scenario played out.

*

One of my good friends, Sharon, is a psychology professor at a prestigious university. She also has a thriving private practice.

Sharon and I were on vacation one day, walking near a beach area that had little traffic and great paved roads that made for a peaceful stroll. As we walked along, I saw something from the corner of my eye. A dog had gotten loose and was running toward the road. As luck would have it, a car was heading right for the dog and didn't seem to be slowing down.

I ran into the roadway screaming "Stop! Stop!" while waving my hands to catch the driver's attention. The driver tried to slow down, but unfortunately the car did hit the dog, but the impact was much less harmful than a head on-collision would have been. Later, I found out that the dog had been taken to the vet, and that his injuries were minor. The dog would be all right.

As Sharon and I sat near the beach, watching the waves lick the shore, she turned to me and said, "How did you know what to do? I was paralyzed."

I thought about it, then said, "I guess, no matter how much knowledge one has (Sharon is highly knowledgeable and respected in her field) there's no substitute for actual experience."

Sharon to this day is one of my closest friends. She had previously been married, and like Lainey and myself, pulled a switcheroo from being heterosexual to being lesbian in her twenties. None of us had any clue when we were growing up that we had any same sex tendencies.

Women often bond and attain lifelong friendships. I'm not sure whether that's because women often dive deeply into their feelings. Even our past female lovers can become our friends again after the hurt and heartache of a breakup has passed.

At the prison unit, Joanna and I became very close. Joanna is totally straight, always has been, but we fell in love as sisters, sharing a deep emotional intimacy and trust, which became the foundation of our decades-long friendship. If either of us is going through a stressful time, we call each other for advice and feedback. Sometimes a friend's honesty hurts, but it's always given from a place of love. Perhaps the best part with close friends is the shorthand we use when communicating with each other: we don't have to provide background information or explain ourselves. We've lived through each other's triumphs, devastations, and fierce roadblocks together. And yes, I've had very close male friends too. Mitch, who I met in graduate school, became like a brother to me.

*

I was supposed to finish two terms of clinical work on the prison unit for my master's degree: January to June, then come back again from September to January. By the end of June, however, I still hadn't been called back to the probation department yet, so I volunteered to stay over the summer as I was learning so much. It was a good decision, because I not only worked on the prison ward, but I was assigned outpatient clients for traditional therapy, as well as work in the family therapy unit. I was always advocating to learn new skills. The hospital experience became my PhD on steroids.

COMING HOME

Just as I graduated from social work school, the city's fiscal crisis ended, and everyone who had been laid off from the probation department returned to work. There were hugs and kisses all around, and I finally was getting paid a living wage again.

The desk in my office with Cece was as I had left it, and I easily slid back into my routines as if the year away had never happened. But I didn't realize how acute my interviewing skills had become from working at the prison unit. One day, after I had finished an interview with a probationer, Cece kept staring at me.

"What? What happened?" I said.

"You should become a district attorney," she said.

"What are you talking about?"

"You took that guy on a roller-coaster ride, asking seemingly innocent questions, then circling back around when he wasn't looking, and nailed him. Wow! He didn't know what hit him."

But I realized the skills I had learned on the prison unit, parsing out truth from fake narratives, now served me well. I decided to take some forensic courses on how to become an expert witness. I had no idea how stressful testifying in a courtroom would be until I actually got subpoenaed by one of my probationers to appear at a trial in which he was a defendant.

CHARLEY

Charley had been assigned to me after being sentenced to probation as a con man. He was the ultimate scammer, he exuded an essence of superior intelligence. He let others know that he merely tolerated our lesser intelligence. *If you're so smart, Charley, what are you doing on probation?* I thought to myself.

He had an old con: he'd pretend he had found a winning lottery ticket on the ground in a parking lot (In reality, he used an old ticket that screamed "Winner!" in large letters across the front.) He whooped it up until an unsuspecting soul, usually an elderly person, came by; then, after using his charm and charismatic skills, he offered to share the winnings with the mark. He'd tell him (or her) that he had to get to work or his boss would fire him—and. if the victim would please turn in the ticket for him, they would share the profits. But of course there was a catch. He needed some cash upfront as a good will gesture to guarantee that the mark would not just turn in the ticket and abscond with the profits. And of course Charley was always the one who absconded with the guarantee money.

When I first met Charley, I realized very quickly he would continue to run his various schemes. When he talked of his crimes, his face lit up as if he had just won an Olympic medal—or, rather, the lottery. The high he got off of scamming people was as addictive as heroin. But drug addicts know their life has spiraled out of control; Charley, in his mind, was too brilliant to ever see his flaws. Maybe his assessment of his intelligence was correct: with all of his prior arrests over the years and numerous suspected crimes, he had only the one conviction for being a con man. Then, while he was under my charge, he got arrested again. And because of his "high intelligence" level, he decided to act as his own lawyer. Hey, he'd seen trials on TV and knew he was as skilled, if not better than, those people.

Charley decided to call me as a witness to prove how good he'd been on probation: he'd kept his reporting appointments, had a good relationship with me, and was working. What he hadn't taken into account was the can of worms that was about to explode in his face.

Walking into the courtroom to testify was nerve-racking. All eyes turned to me—not just from the jury panel but also from all of the spectators in the gallery. There was dead silence as everyone made their assessments of me. I worried, for the first time in my life, how I appeared to others in the room. Had I worn the right clothes? Did I seem competent and professional? I knew two things from my forensics courses: 1) answer questions at my own pace, not that of the questioner, so I could think before I spoke, and 2) answer only the question asked, don't offer additional information.

I was Charley's first witness in his defense. I told the court how cooperative he'd been, that he'd never missed an appointment.

When Charley rested his case, the assistant district attorney took over, and he was good. Despite all I had learned during my forensics training, he pulled thoughts and opinions from me that I didn't even know I had. And so all of Charlie's prior arrests were laid bare for the jury to contemplate. Poor Charlie, the most intelligent man on the planet got creamed by the jury. Quick deliberations! Guilty! Gavel bang! End of story!

THE THREAT

Cece and I had a routine. When either of us were assigned a new case, the other person would stay in the office the first few times the probationer came in for his report, to make sure all was well. After we both agreed that it was safe to be left alone in the office with the probationer, we would then leave the office during the probationer's subsequent reports. Most probationers were well-behaved, cooperative, knowing a misstep could cost them their freedom. As additional insurance, across the small hallway sat Larry in his single office. Larry was a big tough guy who, as a member of the warrant squad, carried a gun: he arrested probationers who had failed to show up for their report or committed other probation violations. Underneath Larry's tough exterior, he was a lovely man.

Cece, Larry, and I became buddies, often going out to lunch together, gossiping about everyone in the building, and laughing a lot (tension relievers were a necessity on every job I worked). Larry was always aware when the rhetoric in our office grew heated: he checked on us to make sure we weren't being threatened in any way. Knowing he was directly across the hall from us provided a safety net for Cece and me.

During my first interview with any probationer, I usually tried to get a sense of the individual and establish a working relationship intent on helping them get their life back in order. I reviewed the requirements for their probation, which might entail: employment, counseling, drug treatment, and restitution payments. I also worked on the goals they imagined for their future. For some people, probation changed their lives. For others, probation was a passing phase until returning to their criminal ways.

I waited until the second visit, after a bit of rapport had been established between my probationer and me, to begin digging into the probationer's deeper personal issues, including family, childhood, and present-day dynamics that may have contributed to their crime.

TINO

I'm so glad Cece was in the office for my first few sessions with Terrance, known in his neighborhood as Tino. He was cooperative, brought in his paystubs as proof of his employment in a mechanic shop, and lived with his older brother in a small apartment uptown. Of course, I verified all of this. During his second report to me, I brought up the subject of his crime. He had been convicted of misdemeanor possession of heroin in his pocket.

"Do you use drugs?" I asked.

"No," Tino replied. "I was holding it for a friend."

"A friend?"

"Yeah, a kid on the street that the cops were chasing. I didn't want him to be busted with dope in his pocket."

"Why were the cops chasing him?"

"I don't know. He was always doing stupid kid things."

"So you were helping a kid who did stupid kid things. Was the kid a drug addict?"

"Don't know."

"So how did you know he even had drugs in his pocket?" Long pause. "Do you use drugs? If you are using drugs I can help get you into a program."

"Me?" Tino said. "Nah, I don't go near that stuff, it'll kill you."

"Could you please roll up your sleeves and show me your arms."

Having worked with drug addicts for many years, I was quite familiar with track marks, evidence of the places in the veins where the heroin-filled needle had been injected. After prolonged use, the veins collapse and other areas besides the drug user's arms are used. I knew of one woman who injected into her mouth, and a man desperate for a fix actually used his jugular vein.

I found no evidence of drug use on Tino's arms, but his story made no sense.

Over the next six months everything went smoothly. Then, Tino was arrested again, this time for beating a man on the street. As he was detained in a local jail, I had him brought to the security room in the courthouse so I could interview him. I had to file a violation of probation report with the court. The report would detail the new arrest; it wasn't a pre-sentence report written after a conviction, just a court notification of a re-arrest.

"Hi, Tino," I began. "How are you doing?"

Tino replied, "Holding up."

"So what happened?" I asked. "You were doing so well, I thought you had the probation thing down pat."

"Yeah, well, this guy was beating this woman on the street so I stepped in to help."

First he saves a neighborhood kid from getting arrested by hiding the kid's drugs, and now he's protecting women on the street? None of Tino's story held together for me.

The next surprise? Tino immediately took a plea, with his lawyer's agreement. What was that about? If he was telling the truth, he had a sound defense. Was he protecting someone else by taking the rap? As he now had a second conviction on his record, probation was not an option; he would eventually be sent upstate to do his time of a few years.

As his supervising probation officer, I was assigned the task of writing his pre-sentence report. I contacted the beating victim for a statement, but he refused to provide one.

To proceed with my report, I went to the assistant district attorney's office to get the facts of the case. As it happened, the assistant district attorney was in her office when I arrived. As I looked through the paperwork, she asked me, "How has he been on probation? Did he give you any trouble?"

"No problem. Followed all the rules. Was a little withholding, but many are, not trusting the process."

The assistant district attorney then said, "I'm going to be recommending the highest prison sentence possible."

That was strange. Except for the two minor offenses, Tino's rap sheet was clean. I'd seen individuals with longer rap sheets given lighter sentences for similar crimes. So I asked, "How come? He only had one other low-level offense. And the current victim was not hurt badly and didn't testify?" A credible victim testifying in a courtroom went a long way toward convicting a suspect and a more severe sentence.

"The victim didn't testify so he wouldn't be killed," The assistant district attorney said.

Killed? What the hell was she talking about?

"You know he's a member of a drug cartel. An enforcer. We suspect he's killed at least two others, but we haven't gotten enough evidence to prove it. Your victim was beaten for committing some low-level offense, otherwise he'd probably be dead. Got to get the message out to others on the street, you know."

No, I didn't know. Who was she describing? Not the guy I'd seen for six months without ever having a problem. There I was applauding myself for all of my newfound skills: being able to lead and conduct interviews, reading body language, understanding a person's essence. Could I have had a murderous cartel enforcer sitting right across from me all of this time?

"Did he ever say anything to you about the cartel?"

I shook my head no as I could not get any words out of my mouth at that moment. How should I process the new information? When I returned to my office, I told Cece what had happened. She'd sat through many of my sessions with Tino. Had she noticed something I'd missed?

"I picked up nothing," she said.

On the prison ward, I'd learned how to separate the detainees who had mental health issues from the fakers. But those individuals were on the unit for thirty days—and they were carefully watched by many individuals over the course of each day. My contact with Tino had occurred in short bursts. I knew I would get over the blow to my self-esteem eventually. Then one day before Tino was sent upstate to serve his time I received a handwritten note from him. I don't remember the exact words of the note, but I do remember the ending. The note itself went something like this:

Dear Officer Mann. Just wanted to let you know that I know everything you've done to me. I'll keep that in mind. I never forget anything. Capiche?

Wait. Wait. Wait. *What you've done to me.* Did he mean *for me?* Had he simply made a grammatical error? And *capiche*? Have any of you ever watched a mafia movie? The word *capiche* often alerts the recipient to an underlying threat of violence. Why would Tino threaten me? Nothing had happened between us. At least not that I was aware of….yet.

Cece and I brought Larry into the office for a private consultation to hear the assistant district attorney's comments and read the letter. We agreed not to discuss the situation outside of the three of us. People would go crazy either thinking I was a hysterical female who didn't belong on the job, or, if they believed the threat was real, the house would come down on Tino, further exacerbating the situation. You *don't* threaten a peace officer. The conclusion of our private office meeting: the threat was real.

Now what? I didn't want to bring the news home to Lainey, but I wasn't myself, and she would know that immediately. Also, as with all couples, our lives were intertwined. I had to tell her.

I started at the beginning. I thought she might get panicky listening to me, but instead she remained calm and spoke in a modulated tone. Remember, she worked on a psychiatric ward.

"Remember my friend Mary from college?" she asked.

Of course I did. She'd visited us several times. I knew she was a social worker living in Boston.

"She's friendly with a forensic psychiatrist. I'll see if she can set us up with an appointment for a consultation."

A great idea. A neutral third party with honed skills to assess the situation.

And so we trekked to Boston, Tino's letter burning a hole in my pocket along with notes I had made on his case so I wouldn't forget any important detail the psychiatrist might need.

Dr. Bernstein was kind enough to see us on a Saturday. Because our meeting was off-the-record, he was relaxed in corduroys and a casual button-down shirt, which helped ease some of the stress in the room. It felt more like a friendly chat than a dire consultation. Mary, who had accompanied us to the meeting, stayed outside in the waiting room so Lainey and I could talk with Dr. Bernstein confidentially.

I went over all of my notes, my impressions of Tino, the assistant district attorney's perspective, the pre-sentence investigation, and finally Tino's note to me. Dr. Bernstein looked down at the letter, turned it over several times even though the underside was blank, and reread the words over and over.

You know when you've had medical tests and the doctor comes in with the lab reports, and you're sitting on pins and needles to see if you're terminally ill? If you've ever had that kind of feeling, you've got this scene.

Finally, Dr. Bernstein looked up.

"You had no conflict with him?" he asked.

"No, nothing."

"Something is missing from this picture," Dr. Bernstein said. "With everything you've told me, there's no reason to target you. Something had to have set him off. Can you think of a triggering event?"

Although I didn't know it at the time, this statement would wind up being the lynchpin that would ultimately save my life.

"So do you think he's serious?" I asked.

He took his time looking over the note again, then lifted his eyes toward me.

"I can't say for sure, and I don't know the triggering event, but based on my gut instinct, yes…I do think this is a real threat."

I don't know whose insides imploded faster, Lainey's or mine.

"What do you think I should do?"

"That answer I don't have."

I thanked him, and Lainey and I went back to Mary's to talk.

Afterward, Mary took us to a local diner to eat. She had seen how upset we were. Lainey kept up the conversation with Mary, as I was basically in a coma. Neither of us had an appetite. On the train ride home, I couldn't shake the nagging question of why Tino was threatening me. After a decent night's sleep, we reviewed our options. Remember, Lainey worked in psychiatry; she understood individuals with compartmentalized personalities.

"Do you agree with the shrink that this is real?" I asked her.

She took a deep breath.

"Unfortunately, yes, I do, even though it doesn't make sense. His evasiveness, the ADA's information, the note, and Dr. Bernstein's interpretation. I think we have to take this seriously."

"Now what? We quit our jobs, leave town, and lose our friendships?"

We decided that when I went back to work on Monday, I would share the consultation information with Cece and Larry and get their feedback. Until then, we tried to enjoy the rest of the weekend. Fat chance. I couldn't sleep, reviewing each detail of the case in my mind. Although Lainey pretended to be okay for my sake, I knew she was just as much of a wreck as me.

On Monday, our private threesome convened in my office. When I finished my tale of our trip to Boston to see the forensic psychiatrist and we reread Tino's note a thousand times, Cece's face took on a sour look, and Larry had sparks shooting from his eyes.

Cece started first.

"You are not going through this alone. Okay? Remember my ex-boyfriend, Peter?" I nodded. "Peter teaches firearms training at the police shooting range. He'll take you to buy a gun that you're comfortable with and train you to use it. And, if I have to get a gun myself, I will. I won't let Tino hurt you."

Then, Larry.

"That motherfucker. That piece of shit. Let him try something. Just let him. I'll take him down myself."

I had never seen this side of Larry, and Cece had stepped right up to the plate, both locked and loaded. Now for the first time in my life, I was paralyzed. What should I do? Was I going to carry a gun around, my nerves on high alert for the rest of my life? I was going crazy. Finally, after tallying all of the votes—Dr. Bernstein, yes; Lainey, yes; Cece, yes; Larry, yes; my subconscious, yes (I already knew the assistant district attorney would vote yes too)—I realized it was a unanimous decision. My life was in danger. I would get my firearms training from Peter. In the meantime, when I left for work in the morning, Larry, armed, would wait for me outside of my apartment building, a few feet away, then follow me from behind in case I was attacked from the rear. I was in charge of scanning the front as I left for work.

The major issue: who would be coming for me? Tino would be in prison…what did his stand-in look like? What a mess. I took a breath Then it finally hit me. *This is real.* I had no choice but to arm myself.

Cece's ex, Peter, took me to the police supply store to buy a gun. We had to select a gun I could handle in my little hand. We found a small-caliber semiautomatic I felt I could control.

As a peace officer, I was legally entitled to carry a firearm. I showed my badge and ID. And so my new life began.

Then, off to the gun range.

I had no idea a shooting range sat in the middle of my old neighborhood. It looked like any other building from the outside. But down, down, down, deep inside the basement and the bowels of the building, sat an entire shooting range, filled with officers taking aim, receiving instruction, cleaning weapons.

You can image the confusion when little me entered the area. I looked like one of the munchkins from *The Wizard of Oz.* But all of the officers knew Peter, and when he explained the situation, everyone was supportive and tried to help in any way they could. When I was ready for target practice and I actually hit my target, the guys cheered for me.

So I learned how to clean the gun, how to assume a correct shooting stance, how to hit my mark on the target. I surprised myself, I was actually a pretty good shot. But target practice wasn't some new sport I was learning.

Peter made that clear: one day, instead of setting up the usual "bull's-eye" target, he put up Tino's mug shot. I turned away.

"Look at him," he instructed. "Even though it won't be Tino, it will be a real human being. And he will be bigger than you. Your only advantage is your concealed weapon. You need to shoot accurately the first time. You may not get a second chance."

Peter taught me to aim at vulnerable parts of the body, but could I actually kill someone…even in self-defense? I didn't know if I could do it. And I wouldn't have the answer to that unless I was confronted and my life was at stake. And then, if I hesitated, I knew I would be dead.

And so my new routines began. Larry following me outside my building, me carrying a concealed weapon.

I felt bad for Larry. Here he was getting up early, leaving his girlfriend in bed, traveling by subway to my neighborhood, just to look out for me. I kept asking if his girlfriend was upset. He assured me she understood. How many more people would be ensnared in my web of fear and terror? How much longer could this go on? I got my answer about a week later.

I was cleaning my gun in our apartment one evening when it slipped out of my hand and fell loudly onto the wood floor. The gun discharged on its own; thankfully there were no bullets inside. But the noise triggered Lainey, who had been the essence of calm up until then. She was suddenly freaking out.

"What if there was a bullet in the gun, either of us could have been hurt or killed!" she shouted. "I can't take this anymore. I just can't. I never know if you'll be coming home, if I'll get a call that you're dead. How long is this going to go on?"

We held each other tightly. I knew I couldn't continue like that either. We lay down to sleep, but all I did was stare at a blank ceiling, my thoughts busting my brain in every direction. Then, I took several deep breaths, held the air in my lungs, and exhaled slowly. The one thought I could not let go of was *Why?* As Dr. Bernstein had asked, what was the triggering event? I had always held this theory: that given enough time, brains will win out over brawn. I needed to know the triggering event in order to get on top of this situation.

As crazy as this sounds, my old theatrical skills kicked in…suddenly I had a plan that might work. I knew I could pull off my part, but Larry would need to be a tougher version of his usual self. I was done being a victim. It was time to reclaim my life. If my plan didn't work, then I guess getting out of town was the only option. Would Lainey join me if I had to run? I couldn't think about that now. I had to make sure Larry and I could pull off my plan first.

The next morning Cece, Larry, and I reconvened in my office. I laid out the details of the plan. Larry was in. Cece thought the plan could work, but had now joined the cast of nervous wrecks. Welcome to the inner sanctum!

Luckily, although Tino had been sentenced, he had not yet been transferred from the local prison to the upstate facility where he was to serve his sentence. I had him brought in from jail to the secure interviewing area upstairs in the court building.

I sat on my side of the cubicle, waiting for the correction officer to bring Tino in. Larry sat on a bench behind me, his badge hanging prominently around his neck, his focus intense, holding an element of anger as if he was about to explode. Tino entered the area. Larry stared straight at him, his eyes never leaving Tino's face, following every step as Tino inched into the room. Larry, the sweetest guy in the world, had suddenly morphed into the most intimidating presence I had ever seen. Tino looked at me, then at Larry, then back to me. I saw not only confusion in his eyes, but for the first time a glimmer of fear.

Tino sat down opposite me, I straightened up and waited. Let his discomfort increase a bit more. His eyes flicked back and forth between Larry and me, his anxiety becoming more palpable. I waited for him to speak first.

"What's going on?" he asked.

"You tell me," I replied. More silence, then I took over.

"You know, Tino, I always liked you. As far as I knew, you and I had never had a problem. I did everything I could to help you get back on your feet and move forward. I felt bad when you got rearrested."

"Yeah, well, shit happens."

I held up the threatening letter and raised it to his eye level.

"You mean shit like this?"

I saw his body shrink a bit. He knew he was in some kind of trouble. I continued.

"After all the time we spent together, after I did my best to help you—and then you threaten me?" He turned his head away. "Look at me…*now*."

He sheepishly raised his head.

"At first I was angry that you could disrespect me when I had always treated you well. But you know what Tino, I was more hurt than angry." That surprised him. "And now, because I still care about you, I'm here to save your ass."

I glanced over my shoulder at Larry. Tino's eyes followed mine.

"You see that man behind me? That's Officer Reyes, my supervisor. He wants you locked up and the key thrown away. Do you know what would happen if he hauled your ass into court for threatening a peace officer, especially me? I know everyone in this building. You think they're going to let you get away with threatening one of their own?"

My voice had lowered at least two octaves. Tino opened his mouth to speak.

"Shut up and pay attention. When you go upstate and the COs learn you threatened me, what do you suppose your life will be like in prison? And especially threatening a woman just doing her job? Your prison time will turn into a hellish nightmare." I leaned in and spoke almost in a whisper. "Now, I told my boss that you would never threaten me. There must be some misunderstanding. He agreed to come and talk to you before reporting you to the court. But first, I need to know why you sent me this fucking letter. And don't you dare tell me it was a mistake."

Tino took a deep breath, looked at me then at Larry. Then back to me.

"I'm waiting," I said.

"You want the truth?"

"That's why I'm sitting here."

"My lawyer told me it was your fault that I'm going to jail for such a long time."

"Did your lawyer explain himself?"

"He told me it was your fault because you put in your pre-sentence report that I should be locked up for the longest possible time."

What the hell? I sat back to absorb what he had just said. So his lawyer, scared of Tino, shifted the blame from himself to me. That lousy bastard. *Well, Mr. Attorney,* I thought, *you fucked up Tino's case, not me.* I had come prepared. I opened a folder I had brought with me and handed Tino the pre-sentence report.

"Here's your report, Tino. Read the whole thing and then read my recommendation out loud."

He slowly scanned each page. He took his time. Sometimes seeing yourself as another perceives you can be an eye-opening experience. Tino finished reading and looked up.

"There's no recommendation."

"That's right. No recommendation. I'm not required to put one down. So as I said, I liked you, so I didn't fill in that piece." (If I was being honest, the assistant district attorney scared me to death.) "Your lawyer lied to you."

"I'm sorry, I'm sorry, I didn't mean—"

"Don't tell me. Tell my boss. He's the one you have to convince."

I stood up and exchanged places with Larry. I could not hear their conversation, but from the look on Tino's face, he'd just been read the riot act: Tino suddenly looked like a guilty little child begging his parent not to punish him. When the talk was over, Larry and I changed places again.

"So, did you work everything out with my boss?"

"Look, I'm really, really sorry," Tino replied. "I know how nice you were to me. I swear I would never hurt you."

"Good to know." And with that, I stood up. Better to leave Tino in a state of agitation, the way he'd left me. "Take care, Tino," I said and walked out.

And with that, Larry and I left. I was free! I was finally, finally free!

Passed the halfway mark of Tino's sentence, I received a call from his prison counselor. He wanted to know if an old warrant of Tino's was still outstanding. I told him no, and we talked for a few minutes.

"How is Tino doing?"

"Very well. He said you helped him a lot."

"Say hello to him for me," I said. "When is he up for parole?"

"Probably around six months from now."

"Well, wish him good luck from me."

"Will do."

Six months. Six months. What if he came back to see me after he got out? Even though I felt confident that Tino would not threaten me again, the trauma had exhausted me. I turned in my gun and decided to change jobs.

MURDERERS, VIOLENCE, VICTIMS

After saying all my goodbyes at the probation department and enjoying a final lunch with Cece and Larry, I cleaned out my desk with a saddened heart and went home to Lainey.

The first weekend, both of us still in shock after my encounter with Tino, we decided to stay home, relaxing, continually reassuring each other that all was well.

That Monday, Lainey went back to work, but I had no job. I needed time to process what had happened and recover from my exhaustion. As I sat snacking on chips and pretzels, drinking tons of coffee and making myself an egg cream, certain insights and patterns emerged from my subconscious.

I'd interviewed many violent perpetrators and their victims; the interactions with these individuals stuck in my mind. I saw particular themes emerge—themes that pertained to certain types of violent individuals. Not the person who snaps under stress in an unusual situation, or the person who commits a misdeed while in the midst of a psychotic episode, or a person who commits a crime driven by a need to take drugs during a withdrawal. No, I mean the type of personality who knowingly, willingly, and in some cases elatedly hurts others by murdering, raping, or committing domestic violence against them.

Recall my mother's words: *The only people who hurt others are those who are hurt themselves.* As I thought about the types of individuals I'd dealt with, a pattern emerged—I'll call it loss of control on the individual's part. But not the loss of control that sometimes occurs during the commission of a crime. No. The loss of control goes way back, usually to childhood. Obviously, no one is born a murderer. What happens? The seeds are sown in front of everyone, only we fail to notice.

The notion of losing control came to me when at eleven years old I witnessed a particular incident. At the time I did not know the significance of the event, nor its impact upon me.

JERRY

Remember the three-story house with the stoop? We lived on the second floor, and Jerry and his family lived on the ground floor. Jerry had no siblings, and we often played together, enjoying each other's company. Jerry's parents were always very nice to me as well.

One day as Jerry and I took a walk around the neighborhood, I heard a horrible, desperate animal sound. When I scanned the empty lot we were near, I saw a small, abandoned, kitten squealing loudly for help.

"Oh no. Jerry, Jerry, look!" I screamed.

I ran over to the pathetic creature and grabbed the trembling baby cat in my arms, trying to soothe her as best I could. She quieted down a bit. I brought the kitten to Jerry.

"Here. You hold her while I go for help, okay?"

And with that, I shoved the kitten into Jerry's arms and ran into the street to flag down help. After a car screeched to a halt, I headed back to the lot, the driver following me. When I got back to Jerry, there was no cat in his arms, only squealing from a sewer drain. I peered through the grate and saw the panicked kitten flailing its legs, trying to stay afloat in the river of city water that engulfed it. My arms were too short to reach through the long opening under the curb, but the driver was able to reach in and grab the kitten. He said he would take her to his vet as he had a cat at home. As he left, I wondered how the cat had gotten into the sewer drain in the first place; it had been nowhere near that area when I handed the cat to Jerry.

I looked at Jerry, who had a self-satisfied smirk across his lips, and the truth dawned on me with repulsion.

"You threw the cat down the drain, didn't you?"

He said nothing. The smirk moved from his lips to his eyes.

"You disgust me," I said as I walked away from him. I swore I'd never speak to him again. But how had Jerry's transformation come about? The cruel, sadistic person who had thrown the kitten down the drain was not the Jerry I knew.

A few weeks later, a letter addressed to Jerry's mother was accidently placed in our mailbox. My mother asked me to bring it downstairs to Jerry's family. I hoped I would not see him. I couldn't stomach looking at his face again.

Jerry's mother answered the door. "This was placed in our mailbox by mistake," I said.

She smiled sweetly, as usual, took the envelope, and made some comment about the sender that I couldn't pay attention to, because torturous screaming was coming from inside the apartment. I sneaked a look around the side of the door, and I saw Jerry being viciously beaten with a belt over every inch of his body. Back then, people hit their kids, but this was beyond ordinary discipline. It was torture. Jerry's screams and pleas for his father to stop were worse than the kitten's desperate cries for help. And there stood his mother, looking over the envelope as if nothing untoward was taking place.

After she thanked me and closed the door, I went outside and sat on the stoop, trying to breathe in fresh air and cleanse my mind. But it was not to be.

As I looked back on that incident, I realized the meaning of *loss of control*. Jerry had no control over his situation. Others who are abused either physically or emotionally, or who watch the helpless abuse of a loved one, have no means to stop the violence. Sometimes to mitigate their feelings, they shut down the vulnerable side of themselves; to regain control of their world, they then set out to abuse others, feeling the power they lost during their own abusive episodes. It's a godlike feeling of redemption and total control.

You've heard of children being cruel to animals or plucking the wings off of a fly? These types of behaviors are not intellectual learning experiences; rather, these acts may be a child's first taste of power, of control over their lives. I kept seeing examples of this loss of control over and over again in the childhood of violent individuals I interviewed or counseled.

I did not know Jerry as an adult, but if anyone was primed for domestic abuse—abuse of his children, or far worse—it was Jerry.

THE VICTIMS

Why do certain fully grown, fully functioning, fully aware individuals become victims of con men and lose all of their money, wind up with partners who constantly cheat on them, are emotionally or physically abused at home, or join cults that sometimes can turn an ordinary individual into a murderer, such as happened among certain members of the Manson gang?

Two elements are crucial here: an inability to validate oneself from the inside, and behavioral reinforcement, which is one of the most powerful human dynamics that takes place in situations where one person dominates another individual.

The behavioral dynamic starts in childhood. Well-meaning parents have to teach their kids how to get along in society. And remember, the children are completely dependent on family for food, shelter, love, and guid-ance. *Do good and I'll reward you with treats*, well-meaning parents implicitly teach their children. *Maybe I'll take you to a movie. I'll hold you and tell you how much I love you and how proud I am of you. Do bad, and I'll send you to your room, maybe not let you play with your friends today, or tell you how disappointed I am in you. Then when you do as I want, the rewards will return.*

That is behavioral reinforcement in a nutshell. We teach our pets to behave through similar means. But the methods of behavioral reinforce-ment can be used for nefarious purposes by those wishing ownership of another person's behavior. As adults we are supposed to evolve as monitors of ourselves. So why allow someone else to assume that responsibility? An inability to be in charge of our self-worth is our weak spot.

As we grow and change through life, coming to know who we are, we choose certain jobs, friends, partners, who match how we see ourselves.

What happens if we can't validate ourselves? If we feel unworthy, perhaps like a loser in life, unable to cope or achieve as others have—then what? We hand over the job of self-worth to another person who we perceive either as having the traits we long for or the power to make us feel as if we do have those traits. Perhaps a charismatic individual steps into your life. Some-one you are dazzled by, who you wish you could be like, or at least share in their limelight. Or perhaps a group that gives you the acceptance you crave— the same acceptance you might not have felt from your family.

Once you give your self-worth to an outside person or group, you are no longer in charge. You may be scammed of all your money for the false promise of love, or the false promises of getting rich and living among the so-called elite. You might wind up in an abusive relationship, join a cult that cuts you, the inductee, off from the rest of the world, including those you love. Competing realities are not tolerated by whoever is in charge of you.

Entering any type of relationship with low self-esteem is a recipe for disaster, as one will always be in a subjugated position. Compromise is neces-sary in any relationship, even friendship; but compromising is different than turning over your self-esteem to another person.

We've all seen the haters trolling the internet—the malingerers who put others down in order to deal with their own insecurities….There is constructive criticism, and then there is negativity spewing from those who have to step on someone else to increase their own self-worth.

We grow, we change, we expand over time, hopefully getting stronger internally. No one is perfect. But the antidote to victimization is self-empowerment, not egotism, not narcissism. Just respect for oneself.

BUBBLE PEOPLE

Did you ever wish you could live in Downton Abbey, or some other rich person's mansion? All of your needs attended to by others. If you got into any trouble, the household's fixers would take care of your missteps and keep you immunized from any consequences. Ah, what a great life!

But is it? Eventually an untoward event will occur, and the bubble will collapse. It might be a slow leak from a pinprick, or a crushing blow sending your insides scattering like debris from a minefield. It might be a sudden loss of wealth when the stock market crashes, or a Ponzi scheme you became caught up in, or an arrest that can't be fixed, or illness, or loss of inheritance. Nothing lasts forever.

Then, what do you do? You're unequipped to handle the inevitable downside of life. Suddenly, your world collapses and you don't have the skills to regain your footing. Your perception of your life—and maybe the lives around you—has been ripped away.

Those with a false sense of self are also ripe for victimhood.

We all have strengths and limitations. Shoring up one's strengths, and perhaps sharing one's wisdom with others, bolsters our self-esteem. Accepting our limitations, even laughing at ourselves, helps others perceive us as authentic and real. There is no greater door opener in life than a natural, authentic person.

WHAT NOW?

After my Tino episode, I needed to go job hunting again, to get settled, to feel a strong foundation under myself once again, back to routines, and a normal life rhythm. I had an interview at a psychiatric hospital (not a prison unit) uptown. I guess the interview went well because the psychiatrist invited me onto the patient unit to follow him around. (Ah. No bars, no corrections officers. But I have to admit I missed the noise and chaos of the prison ward….)

I walked with the psychiatrist through the facility, he talking to the patients, me joining the conversation occasionally. I immediately liked the unit and felt eager to begin my work life again. When we returned to the psychiatrist's office, he had a strange look on his face. Uh oh! Had I overstepped my bounds interacting with the patients? Was I only supposed to watch and listen? Then he said, "I've never seen anyone as comfortable on the unit their first time here."

I actually laughed; then I put a hand over my mouth. I didn't want him to perceive my joy as disrespect.

"Well, it feels like old-home week to me, talking with patients, watching them in the dayroom," I said. "I love this work."

I was sure I nailed it. And then the psychiatrist informed me only a part-time position was open, and it was mine if I wanted it. He added that as soon as a full-time position opened up, he'd offer me that job. I wish he had told me that only a part-time position was open in the first place. There I was all excited and then the rug was pulled out from under me. I declined the offer, because I needed a full-time job. I left. The psychiatrist did call about six months later with a full-time offer, but by that time I was fully employed in an outpatient methadone program at a large hospital in Manhattan.

At the outpatient clinic, there were three teams responsible for seventy-five patients each. The staff for each team consisted of a team leader who was a licensed mental health professional (I was one of the team leaders, as I now had my degree and my license), two paraprofessionals who were former drug addicts, and a nurse who dispensed medication and looked after our patients' health needs. The former addicts taught me street lingo, tips on shooting up and hiding track marks. They shared the devastation drug use wrought on their lives, and I shared clinical evaluations of their patients and suggested treatment plans. Our nurse sat in on all of our team meetings and looked after our patients' medical issues.

Finally, everything in my life had fallen back in place. But as we grow older, we learn that life is in constant motion, filling us with joy, fun—and then sometimes stabbing us with heartache. Given everything I'd been through during my childhood, my sexual coming out, helping volatile and sometimes violent individuals, I thought I was prepared for whatever life threw at me. But sneak attacks can come from anywhere.

So when I observed a slight change at home, I needed to pay attention. Some of our male friends, and even one female friend, seemed to be particularly enamored with Lainey. Yes, Lainey was attractive, subtly sexy, very intelligent, cultured, well-read, but that was just Lainey. If she knew she was being worshipped from afar, she had never acknowledged it.

Now, suddenly, Lainey was responding in a more dynamic, almost intimate fashion to the attention. *What is this about?* I wondered. Was I not enough for her anymore?

I was getting stressed out and nervous. Lainey was my rock, my foundation. I loved her without boundaries. I never knew I had the ability to love another person with such depth, especially after losing my mother and vowing I would never again allow myself to be that vulnerable with another human. And now I was scared.

Lainey and I had been together for more than ten years, having hooked up in our mid-twenties. As far as I knew, we were both monogamous. Prior to becoming a couple, we were each other's only female intimate contact, all other intimate encounters having been with men.

I don't remember how the critical conversation started, but basically Lainey announced that she wanted to try an open relationship.

"We can have sex with others, but that's all it will be. No threat to our relationship."

She looked at me hopefully. She waited. I sat dumbfounded.

Because we had fallen in love unexpectedly, and neither of us had ever previously been with a woman, I understood the desire to find out whether we were lesbians or had simply fallen in love with each other? Did I want to try an open relationship? Absolutely not. Was I terrified of losing Lainey if I said no? Absolutely! It was a classic example of being between a rock and a hard place. I felt I had no choice, so I agreed. My hope? She'd fool around, get bored, and we'd eventually get back to our equilibrium.

And so we went on our new adventures. I knew Lainey had various worshippers lined up. Me? I had absolutely no idea how to go about pursuing my half of an open relationship. My first foray into the new land of sexual freedom started at a friend's house. No, it wasn't with my friend herself, but with a cable TV man.

*

My friend had to work that day, and she asked if I would watch her apartment when the cable man arrived for his appointment. No problem. I got to her place early and let myself in. While I waited for the cable man to arrive, I noticed some pornographic magazines on a bedroom night table. I leafed through the pictures. Images depicting various positions of both heterosexual and lesbian sex popped off the page. The only magazines I'd ever possessed were movie magazines and the TV Guide.

Suddenly, the bell rang.

"Cable man."

"Come on up."

I opened the door to a tall, extremely handsome man, oozing masculinity from every pore. He did not have to flirt. He was already a hot magnet.

I led him over to the TV in the living room so he could repair the faulty wiring, and I hung out to make sure he did not steal anything from my friend's apartment. He then moved on to the bedroom. When he finished the wiring there and turned to leave, he spied the sex magazine on the side table and picked it up, leafing through the photographs.

"You into this?" he said.

"It's not my magazine, it's my friend's."

How lame did that sound? He continued, amused: "Even though it's your 'friend's,' are you into this?"

The flirt was on. I was uncertain what to do next. Do I respond? Do I shut it down? Was I ready for my new open relationship? Why the hell not? It wasn't as if I was going to leave Lainey for the cable TV man, a stranger. This was just about sex, right? So I said:

"I *could* be into this. How about you?"

He smiled with his entire body, and I realized…I was turned on.

"I can take my lunch break now," he said.

"That sounds delicious."

What the hell kind of a flirt line was that? *That sounds delicious?* Really? No Pulitzer Prize winner here.

"I'll go downstairs and tell my boss I'm on break."

"And while you're downstairs, there's a drug store on the corner."

"Got it," he replied.

He came back with a fresh package of condoms. At least he knew how to follow instructions. Wish he had the same fortitude with sex. Here I was about to have my first foray into my new open relationship, and all I kept thinking about was Lainey. What was she doing at home? Who was she with?

Did I enjoy my one-off affair? I have no idea. It went so fast on his part, he could have won a medal for speed sexing. For me, it only left me hungry… but not for him.

Now what? I thought. *Do I tell Lainey? No. No,* I reminded myself. *The rules are we don't tell each other.* So, I called Joanna.

At first she squealed, wanting every detail of my soap opera romance. When I shared the cable guy's "premature" ending, she burst out laughing.

I couldn't believe I'd done what I did. I'd had sex outside my relationship with Lainey. But the excitement turned out to be more intellectual than emotional. The only person I wanted was at home.

At least my first adventure was with a stranger. Was hers? Suddenly I became suspicious of everyone we knew, watching, observing, only half-present in a room. Although we both had agreed to the new terms of our relationship, I realized that once trust between two people is broken, their relationship can never go back to the way it was. I no longer felt snuggled in a protective nest. A hawk was now flying overhead, waiting to pounce on its prey.

*

Adam, a friend of mine from graduate school, kept in touch over the years. A very nice guy, easy to talk to, sensitive to the needs of others. He called one day, and I could hear the upset in his voice.

"My wife left me," he said.

"Oh no! What happened?" I asked. "You two seemed so great together."

"She went off with a woman."

What? Another hetero going rogue. Was this the latest trend?

"Had she ever been with a woman before?" I said.

"No. She said she fell in love with her best friend. That's what happened to you, right?"

"Yes," I said. "Lainey and I never expected to fall in love. It just happened, and now we're in a weird place."

I explained our open relationship and the anguish it was causing me. Nothing beats the emotional security of having friends in the mental health field. Not only do they share knowledgeable insights and know how to really listen, they also understand the need for confidentiality. We decided to meet for coffee and commiserate. Finally, when we were all talked out, we sat exhausted, and just smiled.

"Thank you, old friend," I said, "I needed that."

Then Adam asked, "Would you like to go to bed with me? We're both free for sex right now, and that's all it will be. I know you're with Lainey, and I would never interfere in your relationship. But since we both know each other, and understand our situations, it might be therapeutic."

Hmm? Therapeutic sex? I have to admit that was not on my bucket list. Nor had I ever thought of sex from that perspective. But at least the person making the proposal was someone I could trust, not just a wham, bam, thank you, ma'am. So off we went to Adam's apartment. His wife had moved into her girlfriend's home.

It was the time of free love. At every outdoor concert, couples made out on the grass, had sex in the back seat of cars and in groups on the venue's lawn.

In the hospitals where I worked, I had to open the door to a supply closet very slowly, never knowing if all I would see were shelves of inanimate objects, or writhing bodies in the throes of sex. Oh, if only those supply closets could talk. And, yes, Lainey and I inhabited the supply closet at the detox facility on occasion. I hope the janitor cleaned the place thoroughly.

On one level, sex with Adam was the best hetero sex I ever had. Two hurt people, taking care of each other, both of us in need. We spent a lot of time just talking, holding each other. Some women like rough sex; for me, men who are sensitive to my needs make the best lovers, and that was Adam. I felt enveloped in a cocoon of strength and caring, temporarily protected from the outside battering world.

Adam became my go-to person, not just for sex, but for solace. Then, he shocked me once again.

"Would you and Lainey like to have a threesome?"

I was having enough problems with a twosome, now we had to add another body? Adam had met Lainey once at a party we hosted. Was he also one of the masses attracted to her? Was I just a stepping stone to Lainey? Did anyone want to be with me and me alone besides the cable TV man? Knowing how much Lainey liked new experiences, the wilder the better, I said I would ask her. She jumped at the offer, and we arranged a date for a threesome at our apartment.

Have you ever had sex with an octopus? That's the only way I can describe it. Legs and arms flying everywhere, body parts belonging to whom I didn't know, a total overload of stimuli. I was used to concentrating on one person's needs, not a slew of underworld sea creatures.

Afterwards, Lainey and I agreed we hadn't enjoyed the experience as much as we thought we would. My days of deep-sea sex diving were over.

Adam stayed in my life, more like a healer rather than a hottie. Lainey seemed to be more and more joyful with each passing day. Then, as the old saying goes, "the shit hit the fan."

As I walked down the hallway to our apartment door, I heard raucous laughter and loud intimate giggling coming from inside. Who'd stopped by this time?

I unlocked and opened the door to a "new friend" named Meryl. Both Lainey and Meryl were boozed up, inhaling lines of cocaine. I declined the offer to join in. Meryl was cute, petite, with an infectious camaraderie. I could see Lainey was drawn to her.

I was not much of a drinker; I preferred sleeping at night to carousing in bars. We had a huge fight once, Lainey accusing me of not being fun anymore. I could see that Meryl was the kind of spirit she desired: adventurous, daring, challenging. Meryl became her carousing buddy, I became a third wheel: tolerated, but not wanted.

Lainey and I talked. She wanted Meryl, and she wanted me. I could see all her attention focused on Meryl as I became collateral damage, or maybe an impediment to their wishes. I could not stand another minute of watching their shared joy, and I moved out to the first apartment I found, which was located across the street from our old building.

One day I looked out the window of my apartment and saw Lainey waiting near the curb for a pick up. When the car arrived, I knew it was Meryl. Lainey's whole being lit up, just as it always had for me. Only now, I was just a shadow sneakily viewing my former life through a window across the street.

I moved again. Shortly thereafter, Meryl moved into my old apartment. Lainey and I stopped talking.

I tumbled from a life of love and safety into the jaws of depression. My past traumas reared their ugly heads again. My mother's horrific suffering, my father's quick abandonment of me to a new wife—and now this. The one person I knew would always be there for me was gone.

I was alone. Completely alone. What was the purpose of life if I was to be knocked down and crushed over and over again? I tumbled into a major depression, not knowing whether I would survive my latest fall.

SINGLE AND TRAPPED

So there I was in my new apartment, in my new life, lonely, very lonely, working, but not much socializing. Most of my current friends were an extension of my relationship with Lainey: they were connected to both of us as a couple. What happens in a situation like this? Do friends have to choose between one or the other? Can they be friends with both of us? How would that work? Suppose I shared feelings or information that I didn't want Lainey to know. What position would I be putting my friends in, if they now had to censor their conversations with Lainey so as not to reveal my private thoughts to her?

I had no desire to badmouth Lainey to anyone, so a ghost hung over my conversations. No freedom to speak spontaneously about the breakup, which only increased my loneliness. I knew I needed new friends not connected to my coupledom. But what to do with new friends who did not know about my sexuality?

Back in graduate school, Mitch and Deb and I hung out together all the time. As graduation approached I knew I wanted to remain friends with both of them, but I also knew that would be impossible unless I told them of my relationship with Lainey. I did not want to live a lie with two people, both of whom had become my friends. If I was happy with Lainey, shouldn't my friends be happy for me? So one day, right after graduation, I took them to a nearby park for privacy and fresh air.

"There's something I need to tell both of you."

They turned their full attention to me, knowing something important was coming.

"I'm gay. I'm a lesbian. I've been in a relationship with my partner, Lainey, for several years. I love her dearly, and I'd like to continue our friendships after we graduate, that's why I wanted you to know my real life."

I knew Mitch and Deb would be shocked as they took in the news, because both of them assumed I was straight. Mitch had even asked me out once, but I told him I was involved with someone. He never suspected it was a woman.

Finally, after an interminable pause, Mitch stood up and hugged me.

"I'm happy for you," he said with genuine care. Later he told me that knowing my rejection of him had nothing to do with his looks or personality made him feel better.

Deb presented a different story. She smiled weakly upon hearing my news, but said nothing. Hopefully, she'll come around, I thought. But later, Mitch told me what she had said to him after my reveal.

"How can you still be friends with her? She's sick in the head. She disgusts me."

So there I was, looking for new friends, scared, lonely, and afraid to share certain parts of myself. How do I make friends, real friends, I wondered, when I could not present as a whole person to them?

As things turned out with the friends Lainey and I shared, some stayed with her and drifted from me, others the reverse. Some remained friends with both of us, putting up the walls I talked about and censoring information about her. I really did not want to hear how happy she was with Meryl.

I had one major task to accomplish before I could establish my new personal life; I needed to take back the power I had ceded to Lainey. My self-esteem would now belong to me.

WORK, FUNCTION, WORK

Work was grounding. Jobs where people who are in need count on you require leaving your own problems at the door to be dealt with at another time.

I needed a fully functioning brain at work as I had to think quickly, sift through clients' emotional and behavioral patterns, remain aware of slight shifts in behavior, and find a way to align myself with individuals who were sometimes hostile and suspicious. Going to work, concentrating on my patients, became a respite from the ongoing emotional chaos in my life.

Two important factors for ensuring that a client's therapy is successful are having a trusting, warm relatable relationship with the client, and the client's desire to change.

I saw many clients who showed an ambivalence—and sometimes downright hostility—toward the process. But if they kept showing up, I kept showing up. One man whom I dealt with at the clinic was verbally abusive, always trying to put me down. I let him have his say and never took the bait. I had to be patient and wait until he was ready. One day as I stood up from my chair he commented, "You really are small, aren't you?"

More bait.

"Yes," I said, "but I take up a lot space."

He laughed as he left the room.

REY

Then came Rey. He was in his mid-thirties. He'd been in our drug treatment program for over a year, so most of the staff knew him well. He'd always been a calm and respectful patient.

Our client population was edgy, and at times violence would break out, but we were all trained to handle it. So when the nurses came to tell me that Rey was getting belligerent and abusive at times, that didn't sound like the Rey I knew. They suggested I speak to him, but with another staff member present. I knew that would only exacerbate whatever was going on.

I had a good relationship with Rey, so I was not nervous when he came to my office.

"Hi, Rey," I greeted warmly. "How are you doing?"

Rey replied, "All right."

"The nurses have been worried about you," I said.

He looked at me, curious to hear my next statement. His posture tightened as if he was getting ready to defend himself. I continued.

"I've seen the change myself. You're angry and aggressive and almost had a fistfight with another patient the other day. What's going on?"

Rey shrugged his shoulders.

"C'mon, Rey, let me help you. I know you're struggling with something. You've talked to me about everything else in your life. Why won't you trust me now?"

He looked down and cupped his forehead in his hands.

"Rey?"

His usually loud, confident voice now had an almost mousy quality to it.

"I'm not sure," he said. "I feel weak, sometimes I forget things—names, you know—and sometimes I forget how to do things. I lose my balance at times. It's scary. I don't know what the hell is going to happen next. I'm sorry. I didn't mean to act like such a shit."

I asked him a few more questions and almost wished I hadn't. There are times in life when we pray to be wrong. Unfortunately, my prayers were not to be answered. I talked to our team nurse and our team doctor and shared my concerns. Rey had a full workup, head to toe. Unfortunately, my fear was correct. Like my mother, Rey had a brain tumor. He was only thirty-five years old and alone in the United States. His parents still lived in his country of origin.

Surgery to remove Rey's tumor was scheduled for a Monday morning. I went to see Rey at the hospital the Sunday before.

When I looked into his room, Rey was lying in bed, his eyes staring up at a blank ceiling.

"Hi, Rey."

He turned toward me.

"Hey, hi." His whole being lit up. "I wasn't expecting you."

"How are you doing?"

"I don't know. They're giving me these pills so I don't feel too much. The surgery is tomorrow."

He sat up straight and looked at me. I sat down next to him and truthfully did not know what to say. I saw the hope in his eyes and would never rob him of that. But part of me was back in my childhood, where hope was nothing but a cruel tease.

"Can I get you anything?" I asked.

I figured going to the nurses' station or vending machine would give me time to get my act together.

"Can I ask you for a favor?" he said.

"Sure, what do you need?"

His response was something I never expected, and it shattered my heart.

"Will you go to the day room with me?"

"Of course, if that's what you want. But we won't be able to talk privately there."

"I know."

Again he hid his head in his hands as if repelling tears from his eyes.

"Everyone has visitors on the weekend except for me. I...I...." He searched in his head for the words.

"Take your time," I said. "I'm listening."

"I just want them to see that someone cared enough to visit me too."

Seeing Rey so vulnerable, scared and needy, pulled my guts apart. I was already so vulnerable from dealing with Lainey's breakup and Rey's diagnosis returning me to my childhood.

"Let's go," I said, smiling at him.

We headed to the day room and agreed, for confidentiality purposes, that he would introduce me as a friend from his neighborhood. The dayroom was filled with chatter above the surface and trepidation below. Rey and I talked with the others, and every time I felt him slipping away, I covered for him, telling others his lack of focus was from the medication, as I continued talking to the group. Then, visiting hours ended, and Rey walked me toward the elevators, stopping near an office door before reaching the elevator bank.

"Thank you for coming," he said. "I have one more favor to ask."

"Sure. What is it?"

"Can you give me a hug?"

The clinic had a "no touching" policy. Was this a time to break the rules? What would happen when he returned to the clinic? Would it be awkward? But he was obviously terrified and just wanted to be held, even if for only one minute.

"I'm sorry, Rey. I can't. But I'll stop by and see you again after your surgery—and everyone at the clinic is sending you their best wishes and looking forward to your return."

A few days after Rey's surgery, he died, never having regained consciousness. It's been years, but I'm still haunted by my decision to deny him that hug…that last act of humanity.

KEVIN

Whether in a hospital with detoxing men, a psychiatric ward, a prison, or even an outpatient detox unit—all places where men in volatile situations cope with emotional whiplash, bodily changes, and, sometimes, episodes of mental illness—unexpected violence can break out at any time. And it almost always comes out of the blue. No matter how trained my fellow staff members and I think we are, every crisis is unique.

One day at the outpatient methadone clinic, I was suddenly confronted with an unusual situation that I had not read about in any training manual. True, there were certain techniques I had learned and could apply to my sessions with patients. If a patient becomes agitated, the calmer I am the better, even if I'm freaked out. If I convey anxiety or fear, doing so merely escalates the patient's difficulties. Trust is essential in these situations. If a patient knows me, and if we've had positive interactions previously, hooking into our previous dynamic greatly assists the situation.

Kevin had been at the methadone clinic for over two years. He was a large man who could have been a linebacker for the New York Giants. I mean, he was *big*. After I received a call from Lisa, a nurse at the clinic, that a problem had arisen on the unit, I ran over to her end of the clinic, where I found Kevin barricaded and crouching behind a desk he had turned sideways. He was using the desk as a shield for whatever danger he believed himself to be in. Lisa was in the nurse's station. Fortunately, the clinic had closed for the afternoon so no other patients were present.

Kevin was breathing raggedly, his eyes and ears primed to pick up any signals indicating danger. I knew the slightest misstep could set him off.

Lisa, an experienced nurse who was my size, seemed composed, even though I knew we were both freaked out.

"Hi, Kevin," I said, "what's going on?"

"They're after me," he said, wildly scanning the room. He finally turned toward me. Fortunately, he recognized me. At the moment we were safe.

"Who's after you?" I said softly.

"There's a contract out on me. They're gonna kill me today."

Who or what was about to assassinate him, I didn't know, but I needed to find out, and quickly.

"Kevin, I want to help keep you safe," I said. "You know that, don't you?"

He nodded.

"Can I come closer so that we can talk?"

I did not want to invade his territory without his permission, and I wanted him to feel as if he had some control over the situation, even if it was only over the space behind the desk barrier.

Kevin indicated that I could move toward him. I moved slowly, his eyes evaluating my every step, a reassuring smile on my face.

"Kevin, tell me who's after you so Lisa and I can be on the lookout."

No response. So I continued: "Is it a drug dealer?"

He shook his head no.

"Do you owe money to someone?" Again, no response. "Did you see this person today? Can you describe him so we'll know what he looks like?"

Kevin started shaking like a two-year-old who'd been scared by a Halloween ghost.

"It's the vibes. I can feel him. He's nearby," Kevin said.

"What does he want?"

"To hurt me. He's sending signals into my brain."

Uh oh. Good news and bad news. It didn't sound as if a real person was going to break into the clinic and attack us, but at the same time, a psychotic break can be just as dangerous, especially with only two small women and an oversized man in the room.

"Do you know where the signals are coming from?"

I knew enough not to deny his "reality" as that would only cause more agitation.

He pointed above him, toward the sky.

"All right," I said. "Let Lisa and I talk so we can come up with a plan to keep you safe."

Oh, shit, I thought. How were we going to get out of this? Kevin was a really nice guy who had a family and who had never exhibited symptoms of mental illness. Nor had his wife ever spoken to us about unusual behavior. Was this Kevin's first episode? Was it somehow related to a new drug he'd taken?

Either way, we had to deal with what was in front of us.

Lisa was great. We both projected a calm air as we talked over our options.

We needed to get Kevin to the ER, where he could be medicated and eventually transferred to the psychiatric unit, but how would we get him there? If we called security to take him to the emergency room, the sight of the guards might lead to more agitation. But the ER was two buildings away; we couldn't get him there without security. Trying to do so would be too dangerous.

The two of us alone could not walk Kevin down several hallways filled with strangers. If he decided one of the strangers was the assassin, the situation could explode. Who would protect the stranger? Who would protect Lisa and me?

Shit! I really didn't know what to do, and there was no time to phone someone for advice. He was too volatile.

"Kevin," I said calmly and sweetly, with a smile, "we have a plan to keep you safe. Can I come over and talk to you?"

No response, just desperation oozing out of him.

"Kevin, I need you to look at me and tell me it's safe to come talk to you."

He slowly looked at me then said, "Yes. It's safe."

I walked nearer to him and lowered my voice so he'd have to concentrate on my words. He leaned in.

"I know how upset you are. Lisa and I want to keep you safe. I personally know some of the security guards. They are my friends." (Not true.) "Let me talk to them about the best way to get you to a safe place in the hospital, okay?"

"Yes, yes," Kevin said. "Okay."

"All right, I need you to take deep breaths while I set this up and count backwards from one hundred in between breaths…Can you do that? It'll help calm you down while we work everything out."

I had no idea if my plan would work. I hoped if he had to concentrate on his breathing and the numbers, it might distract him from the voice inside his head and buy us time.

Kevin began the exercise. Lisa helped coach him. I ran out to the hallway and called security, explaining I needed men who had experience with psychotic episodes and a supervisor to run the operation, and they needed to arrive quickly.

The security team was there in a flash, thank God. I did not know Sergeant Mendez well, having only said hello to him in the hallways. But I explained the situation, and he said he understood.

"Most important to remember," I told him, "he thinks you are here to protect him. Maybe you guys could act like Secret Service, with an advance man to clear the hallways in front, as if for his benefit even though it's really to keep the visitors safe."

"No problem," the sergeant replied.

"And most important, don't touch him or talk to him. He's used to me and Lisa, but I don't know what your voice or touch will trigger in him."

"We got you," he said; then he smiled at me. "You're doing a great job," he said. I was so grateful for the support, I almost burst into tears.

The other seven men nodded in agreement. The eighth man was already clearing the hallway ahead.

I went back inside. Lisa and Kevin were breathing and counting together.

"Okay, it's all set up," I told Kevin. "They know what's happening and will make sure no one gets near you while we get you to a safe place."

I smiled at Lisa, grateful for her help and her skills. I was expecting to go by myself but then she said, "I'll come with you." I was thrilled to have her by my side.

"Kevin," I said, "you and Lisa keep doing the breathing and counting, and I'll handle the rest."

We stepped outside. Kevin stopped, scanned the men. I felt the fear welling up again inside him.

"Kevin, this is Sergeant Mendez," I said, introducing the sergeant. "He's a friend of mine. He'll take good care of you, and Lisa and I will be with you every step of the way."

Following my instructions, Sergeant Mendez only nodded and said nothing. Kevin did not move.

"The guards are going to put us in a protective circle as we walk down the hallway," I explained. "If you feel nervous at any point, just tell me, and we'll scout out the situation before we advance further, okay?"

Finally, Kevin walked hesitantly forward. He, Lisa, and I moved to the center of the circle as the guards closed ranks around us but remained at a safe distance. They made sure not to accidentally touch Kevin. Lisa and Kevin continued the counting and breathing exercise. Our little group looked like an alien organism moving as one down the corridor.

We made it down the hallways and arrived safely at the emergency room. I thanked everyone profusely and headed inside with Kevin, walking over to a small examining room. He sat down on the bed, already quieted by the lack of stimuli around him.

"Let me talk to the doctor and I'll be right back."

Dr. Dorman was in charge. She was a young doctor, seemed competent and listened intently to me. I don't know how much psychiatric experience she had, but I was about to find out, and not in a good way.

"I'll sit with him awhile," I said, "you come in with the meds, and I'll stay with him while the medicine takes effect. Please, just act warm and friendly, he's very paranoid right now."

I went back inside the patient room. Kevin seemed calm and more able to listen. Dr. Dorman entered.

"Kevin, this is Dr. Dorman."

"Hi Kevin," Dr. Dorman smiled.

Then I spoke to Kevin again. "I've asked Dr. Dorman to give you some medicine to help you calm down. I know how anxious you are. But you're in a safe place. No one can hurt you in here. Is it all right for her to give you an injection?"

Kevin looked at Dr. Dorman and the needle. Then he looked back to me. I gave him a nod of assurance.

"You'll feel much better very quickly, and then I can take you to a safe space so you can get some sleep, okay? And I'll be with you every step of the way."

Dr. Dorman gave him the injection, what it was I don't know, but I hoped it would work quickly. And then she made a horrible rookie mistake.

As she left the room, she locked the door behind her. You never, *never* lock a staff member in a room with a psychotic patient and no means of escape. What if the medication didn't work as intended? What if the patient incorporated me into his delusion and decided I was the one who'd been sent to kill him? I'd be dead in two seconds flat.

Fortunately, the meds worked quickly: Kevin lay back down on the bed. When Dr. Dorman came back to check on us, I was furious but said nothing.

Eventually the guards returned, and we escorted Kevin up to the psychiatric ward. I sat with him in the quiet room as he finally fell asleep. Then, exhausted, I headed home.

KATIE

And then there was Katie. Strap on your seat belts…make sure they're nice and secure!

Katie was in her twenties, very attractive, physically fit. She'd been clean for over six months. Told me she was a "server" at a local restaurant and club. Me being naïve in certain areas, I thought that meant she was a waitress. One day, she comes in complaining about dizziness, loss of balance, numbness in several parts of her body. *Oh no, please God, not another brain tumor,* I thought.

"When did this start?" I asked.

Katie had a habit I had noticed. When she was reluctant to tell me information she thought might make me judge her, she looked down then stuck her tongue out to moisten her lips and front teeth. She was completely unaware of her "tell."

"Katie?"

The tongue came out and wet her lips again; then, finally, she looked up.

"I'm a sex worker. I work in a private, high-end club."

Okay. A lot of the female addicts prostituted themselves on the street for drug money, or worked in higher end escort services.

It's not like I had never heard of sex clubs. My friend Mitch from graduate school had gotten divorced right before first semester started. He attended these sex clubs and invited me to go with him one night. Of course, I wasn't going to miss out on a new experience like this. The clubs were under-the-radar events that one had to know about; not strip clubs. These clubs catered to various outlier activities.

What Mitch did not tell me was that after drinks and food, the "show" did not start until midnight. I had to work at seven the next morning, so I didn't know whether I could sit through all, but Mitch said he'd fill me in if I had to leave. The show started on an actual stage; later, for those who wanted more, private rooms were provided in back. I thought the audience would be all male, but many women attended. Apparently, the sex club was a turn on for couples who were into the same activities as the ones being performed onstage. . The business was cash, providing anonymity, I supposed, and the club charged a hefty entrance fee.

When the show started, it primarily consisted of bondage and discipline: whips, chains, cuffs, spankings. Unfortunately, I had to leave after Act One. Act Two, Mitch told me later, was role play. Role reversal, costumes, teacher and misbehaving student. Okay. But the next one got me: a man dressed in just a diaper being fed by a mother figure whose lap he occupied. Sometimes he took nourishment from a bottle, other times from her breasts. Then, some men acting as dogs on a leash. My feeling has always been, if you and your partner are consenting adults and the sex isn't dangerous, have fun.

The women I saw performing at the club before I left had a raw sexuality about them. Katie did not. In fact there was a certain elegance in how she flowed into a room. I had trouble visualizing her in one of these clubs.

"So what exactly do you do at the club?"

"Well..." she said, hesitant to speak. Finally, she looked away and resumed: "The men lie on the floor naked. I dance over them, taking off my clothes, dropping them below, then spread my legs on either side of them, and pee up and down their bodies. Their faces are covered in a see-through plastic shield, preventing the urine from splashing their eyes."

"Golden showers," I said, wanting her to know I'd heard about this before.

"I get great tips, make a lot of money. The bad part, I have to drink a lot of fluid so I can pee constantly."

"Okay, so did anything change at work?" I kept my voice as neutral as possible.

Her tongue returned, perusing her lips. I waited.

"They brought in this contraption a few weeks ago. It's sort of like a trapeze. Now I ride over the men with my legs spread apart so they can see up my vagina. Then, I turn upside down on the swing, my breasts dangling near their faces, while they reach up and try to lick my nipples."

I'd been to the American Ballet, and can say with assurance that I'd never seen a move like the one Katie was describing.

"Katie, I'm not totally sure about this," I said, "but there may be something in your new routine that could be causing your symptoms. We need to

rule out any underlying medical conditions. You know Pam, the nurse prac-
titioner in the medical office? I think you need to see her for an evaluation."

"No, I can't see her." Fear of judgment from other people was often a
difficult wall to scale.

"Look," I assured her, "I know Pam really well. She never makes judgments, never divulges any information except medical diagnoses and medication updates. I can make an appointment and go with you if you like."

"Okay, if you go with me," Katie replied.

The next day, we went to see Pam. Katie shared her symptoms with
her, but she was reluctant to share the activities that might be the underlying
cause of her physical problems.

"Would you like me to tell her about your job?" I asked her.

She nodded her permission.

As I started to explain the situation, Katie suddenly took over. As she
shared the intimacies of the job with Pam, I saw Katie take ownership of her
life, the level of shame peeling away one sentence at a time.

Pam sent Katie for some neurological tests, all of which came back
negative. Then Pam warned Katie that if she did not stop her new activities
at the sex club, she might permanently damage herself. And so she stopped.
She still worked at the club though.

On some level I think Katie liked teasing the men lying on the ground,
making them beg for what they wanted. Her own past had been dominated by
a rigid father who had strict expectations of both Katie and her mother. At the
sex club she had a taste of playing the opposite role. Being the one in control.

Starting at a young age, certain patterns and themes dictating our
behavior become common in our lives. Often, these themes continue into
adulthood, as we remain unaware we've ceded control of our lives to the
forces that gave rise to the past themes. If, as was the case with Katie, someone in our past had dominated our lives, we might pick a similar person to be

our life partner when we are an adult and thus remain abused. Or we might break the original pattern and do the opposite, as Katie had done to become the dominant partner in the sex club. Either way, we're still being controlled by the past until insight is gained on a conscious level and we begin to make decisions as an adult in the present.

THE TURNAROUND

Having been in a relationship for so long, I had no idea how to date, and I did not want to get blasted again, I was still too vulnerable.

Adam, my octopus-sex partner, continued to have sex with me as a twosome. Was he the one? Of course not. He was my teddy bear, providing respite and comfort in a time of great upset. Perhaps I provided the same for him following his divorce.

I went to several lesbian events in the city, met some lovely women, and made dates to get together at a diner for coffee or see a movie. It was fun, but not satisfying.

Bev, a friend of mine held a New Year's Day get-together every year; she always invited a fun group of lesbians. Some coupled (as Lainey and I were at that time), some single, some in the midst of breaking up. Bev loved setting up the single lesbians with each other. Her matchmaking skills, even today, remain legendary.

Lainey and I loved Bev's parties. They were the only time during our relationship when we switched roles. Lainey would talk and gossip with everyone sitting on the sidelines, and I'd hit the dance floor. I danced with everyone, one-on-one, twosome, group—even by myself if everyone else was tuckered out. Maybe breaking out on the dance floor was the antidote to being calm and buttoned-down all week at work where my focus was always on the patients, dealing with other people's traumas and sometimes, death.

Stepping away from the dance area, I noticed a petite, pretty woman staring at me. Did I look too crazy out on the dance floor? But then I felt a sadness emanating from her.

During a phone call with Bev after the party, I found out that the woman's name was Constance, or Coni, as she preferred, she was in the midst of a difficult breakup. She came to the party alone to get out of the house; her partner had remained at their apartment. I felt bad for Coni, but it made me even more grateful that I had Lainey in my life and in my heart.

Six months after Lainey and I broke up, I was still looking for friends who were not connected to us as a couple. I remembered Coni and asked Bev to give her my number if she ran into her. I reiterated that I was looking for friends, not a relationship. I heard nothing for months and forgot about it. Then, out of the blue, Coni called.

"How are you doing?" she asked.

"Starting to get out somewhat," I said. "And you?"

"Same."

We talked a little more, sharing our relationship and breakup stories. Then, I don't know who said it first, we decided to have brunch together on Sunday. She lived in the suburbs, didn't get into the city much, but thought it would be a nice change of pace. I knew a restaurant where a lot of lesbians gathered and the food was good. So that Sunday she met me in front of the restaurant. This time she was smiling.

Sometimes you meet someone and it takes a while to feel comfortable with them, but they can turn out to be one of your lifelong friends. Other times you click right away. One of the signposts for me is laughter: it shows the two of you share a similar sense of humor. It's the human drug of health, healing, and happiness, and Coni and I laughed a lot.

After the meal, I thought Coni would head back to the "burbs," but she said she had time, and we walked around the West Village for a while, landing at my favorite place: fresh soft-serve ice cream. What better way to make a new friend then to slurp and lick in unison?

We had one important thing in common: Coni was a special procedures X-ray technologist working in the cardiac care unit of a local hospital where human beings lay on a table while having blockages removed from their arteries. Sometimes the procedures did not go as planned, despite the doctors' best efforts. Blood splattered all over the surgery room, and on masks, gowns, and gloves. The patients' families waited outside to hear the good news announcing the procedure had been a success. But sometimes they were met with the grim news of loss.

Coni and I understood each other's work life. So when the ice cream slurping finished, I invited her to my apartment to talk further in a quiet environment.

Back at my apartment, we laughed a lot more. I felt a weight lifting off of me, and took a deep breath of fresh air. Then, I panicked. I had a date coming over in half an hour. Even though Coni and I were just friends, I didn't think it would be a good look to have another woman in my apartment when my date showed up. It wouldn't have been a big deal if Coni had been a relative, a neighbor, a best friend; but I'd just met her, and we had slurped ice cream together. I didn't think that explanation would fly.

"Listen," I said. "I have a date coming over. Sorry, do you mind—"

"Oh. Okay," Coni said. "No problem." She got up to leave.

"I'll give you a call," she said.

"Please do," I replied.

And with that I hoped I had a new friend. The next day, Coni called.

"How was your date?"

"Hmm, not sure yet."

That lovely laugh rolled down her tongue. I could visualize the glint in her eye that accompanied her laugh. Is it possible to flirt on the phone? I'd never thought about that before.

"So, when can we get together again?" she asked.

"Wait, let me check my schedule….Hmm, you're not going to believe this, but my weekends are booked for the next five weeks."

"Boy, you are busy."

"I guess I don't want to sit here thinking of everything I've lost."

"Yeah, I understand. Well, let's talk on the phone for now and book me in after the five weeks."

We became very close and intimate on the phone. Just the deep sharing women do after they learn to trust one another. Finally, the five-week hiatus ended. This time, I called her.

"How about this weekend?" I asked. "The weather looks great."

"Yeah, I know. I want to take you to my grandmother's house."

There was a pause, mine, that exploded into the Grand Canyon.

"Are you okay?"

How many of you have gone on a possible first date to Nana's house? There were only two reasons I could think of to go to Coni's grandmother's house. One, her grandmother was someone famous and Coni wanted to keep it a secret until I saw her. Two, Coni really wasn't into me, and we really were just going to grandma's house.

Whoa, baby! This was a new one on me. After my gigantic pause, Coni said, "My grandmother lives at the beach. You walk out the back door, and there it is. It's beautiful, and it's private. I thought you might enjoy a day at the beach."

When I was a kid, my private beach was my towel and the towels of two of my friends on the crowded beach of Coney Island. We would have defended our private beach with our lives.

"My grandmother lost her husband early on," Coni explained. "She supported herself working in the bra department at Macy's."

Nope, didn't sound famous.

"Then she met a man who owned this beach house. They married, and when he died, she inherited the house."

"Great," I said, "let's go to the beach."

"I'll pick you up at the train station, we'll drive to my grandmother's, and then we'll come back here. There's a nice restaurant near me where we can have dinner."

"Okay, I'm in."

Later that day, as Coni and I walked up the pathway to Grandma's, wow, I couldn't believe it. I know this sounds trite, but as a kid who never went anywhere except Coney Island, which was invariably raucous and overcrowded, I was immediately enchanted with the private beach outside Grandma's back door. Seagulls winged overhead, screaming to each other, the smell of fresh salt water filled my lungs, and I listened to the mesmerizing sounds of waves flapping on the shoreline. I wanted to stay there forever. But wait. First, I had to impress the family.

Besides losing my mother as a kid, I'd also lost my maternal grandmother, whom I loved dearly. My Nana was a big, bundle of mush, with a wicked sense of humor. When I stayed overnight, my grandfather, a mailman, went to sleep early. Nana and I would stay up late, which I wasn't allowed to do at home. She told me jokes, and we'd laugh uproariously, especially at my grandfather, whose snoring reached scales unknown at the Metropolitan Opera House.

Coni's nana had that type of essence. The moment I met her, I felt totally comfortable. No need to impress anyone. Just be myself. And Nana's sense of humor, dirty jokes flying from her lips. And wait…there's more. Unlike my Nana, who cooked Jewish food (remember the brown, green, and white bricks?) this Nana cooked Italian food from scratch. If I was in a 1930s movie, I'd be swooning now. And guess what we were having for lunch that day: homemade lasagna. Had I hit the jackpot, or what? Coni? Who's Coni? Forget her, I was ready to move in with Grandma.

Soon enough, there I was, scooping up mounds of lasagna, laughing my head off, ignoring Coni, until she finally said, "Don't you want to go the beach?"

The beach? The beach? And walk out on Nana?

"Of course," I said.

I couldn't be impolite, could I? The house was a small, prefab with three bedrooms, two baths. I was assigned a room to change into my bathing suit then off we went: umbrellas up, folding chairs in place, towels awaiting our dip in the ocean. Just Coni and I, no other beachgoers, no ice-cream venders yelling about the latest flavor, no strangers sleeping next to us on blankets.

For the first time since my mother's death and Lainey's abandonment, I felt peace inside myself. How long would the feeling last?

When the day ended, Nana and I hugged goodbye as if we'd known each other for decades, and Coni and I headed for her neighborhood and the restaurant she'd talked about earlier. We spent the car ride sharing stories of our childhood; and when we arrived at the restaurant, everything changed. We ordered, we smiled, we ate…well, sort of. I ate, she toyed with her food.

"Is something wrong with your food?" I asked.

Coni smiled weakly and shook her head no. I thought we had had a great time. Maybe, after considering the whole day, she'd had enough of me. *Oh, well, here we go again,* I thought. I had opened the door to let some light in and was about to get it slammed in my face.

Then: "Would you like to see my house? It's small. I just bought it with money I'd saved, and a big mortgage. You can meet my cats, TJ and Blondie."

Yes! I was back in. What is more intimate than meeting someone's cats? Little did I know just how intimate meeting her cats was about to be....

*

Coni's home was a nice compact two-bedroom on a quiet block, if you don't count the parkway nearby with its *zoom, zoom, zoom* of cars zipping by. Modern life's equivalent of a nighttime symphony of cicadas, only with gas fumes and honking horns.

Inside, the cats came to greet me. Of course, you never know if certain cats you've just met are greeters or security guards protecting their property. Both were adorable. I bent down to pet TJ, who rubbed circles around my legs, but Blondie backed away.

"Be careful with Blondie. She's shy, and if you pick her up, make sure her tail is underneath her."

"Okay," I replied.

"She has anal gland problems," Coni explained.

Hmm. I wasn't expecting us to get this intimate this quickly.

"Even though I just ate, tell me anyway. What the hell is an anal gland problem?"

"She shoots liquid out of her ass every once in a while. It's not diarrhea, so don't worry. I took her to the vet and he said not to do anything unless it gets worse. Then she may need surgery."

I nodded, but said nothing. What is the polite response to shooting anal glands?

I followed Coni downstairs to a small finished basement with a fire-place and a separate laundry area. Coni had the fireplace prepped and ready. She lit the logs and put on a Lionel Richie album. We sat next to each other quietly listening to Lionel's romantic, melodious tones.

"How come you stopped talking to me in the restaurant?" I asked.

"I was choking on my food."

"Why didn't you signal for help?"

"It wasn't that kind of choking. I was nervous. I wanted so badly for you to like me, I couldn't eat."

I became hysterical laughing.

"It's not that funny."

"Oh yes, it is."

I'm not going to share with you the details of how we got from the romantic scenario in the basement into the bed upstairs. Finally, it had been a long day, and we snuggled in for a good night's sleep.

I awoke in bed the next morning thinking I would puke. No, it wasn't the restaurant food from the night before, it was Blondie's anal glands, which she'd obviously shot off during the night. It was the foulest smell I'd ever encountered in my life. And there was no hiding from it. The aroma pervaded the blanket, the air, and all four walls of the bedroom. I shook Coni awake.

"What's wrong?" she said. "Oh, God, Blondie shot off again…."

We scrambled out of bed as fast as we could. I hopped in the shower, Coni searched for a now hidden Blondie to wipe her ass. When all was well, we sat in Coni's breakfast nook, drank coffee, and laughed our heads off. Some first date, huh? But it wasn't over yet. As we left the house so I could go back to the city, we opened the front door and found a skunk had shot off on the front lawn. If ever the powers that be wanted to send me a message, this was it. Ass smell to the front of me, ass smell to the back of me…Was there ever a more alarming omen to heed? But, as usual, I didn't pay any attention to the signs and forged ahead.

STUMBLING BLOCK

I continued to see Coni. But Blondie was a problem. No, not because of her anal glands. I figured after living through the first shocking wave of Blondie expressing herself on Coni's bed, I would survive other emissions. But Blondie wasn't warming up to me. Did she not like me, or was she upset that I had coopted her side of the mattress? I love animals, and I really wanted to be Blondie's friend, but every time I approached her, she ran and hid under the bed.

I thought exhaustively of how to handle Blondie. I had had one other experience with a cat who hadn't been friendly. Following my first few months after graduating from college, I had saved enough money to rent a small walk-up apartment. It was the first time I had private space all to myself. I loved it, but at times felt lonely coming home from my first job, no one to greet me, no one there to share my day.

At that time, a friend of mine from college was still living at home, a home with a backyard. She too loved animals and had started feeding a feral cat on a daily basis. But her mother had allergies and would not allow the cat inside. She'd named him, Alley, as in *alley cat*, and asked if I would take him.

Winter was approaching, so of course I said yes. A loving pet to come home to, I thought…Boy, was I wrong.

He was a tough boy, I was a tough girl. We had a big problem.

But he was so beautiful, gray, sleek fur, deep yellow eyes possessing the heightened alertness of a wild, abandoned animal left to fend for himself. He watched my every move, alert for danger, constantly deciding whether I was worthy of living with him. I felt stalked in my own apartment. I fed him and kept my distance. He seemed ready to pounce at any wrong move. If I got too close, he'd hiss, like a snake warning off a threat. Other times, he'd bare his teeth. A few times he did bite me. Nothing needing a doctor, but still scary and unpredictable.

I knew from working at the inpatient drug detox hospital—a facility with men who had to survive on the streets and men who had survived prison life—that I had to be patient, not react, and be especially calm if I was going to win Alley's trust. But Alley and I had a big problem: a property dispute.

I had splurged on one item in the apartment, a comfy TV chair. There was also a secondhand couch for friends that faced the opposite living room wall, but there was only one chair that faced the TV.

Every night after dinner, Alley took up residence on my TV chair. The couch would have been just as comfortable for him, but no, I think he knew the chair was my throne, and he let me know who was really in charge. And so began a nightly ritual: I asked Alley nicely to vacate the chair, he refused, and then I'd pick him up and place him on the rug. He'd hiss, bare his teeth, and sometimes nip at me. Finally he'd give up, saunter to the couch and jump on top of it. Then we both sat in our places, eyeing each other and waiting for the other's next move. I'd talk to Alley lovingly, always in a mellow tone.

"Alley," I'd say, "there's nothing to be afraid of, sweetheart. This is your home. You're safe here with me, and I'll always take care of you."

Talk about falling on deaf ears. A few of my friends, knowing the situation, advised me to take Alley to a shelter. But I'd never given up on my patients no matter how much they acted out, and I sure wasn't going to give up on Alley.

Our tension-filled routine lasted for weeks. Me putting Alley on the rug, Alley hissing and snarling at me then jumping onto the couch.

One day, I again lifted Alley off my chair and placed him down on the rug, but this time he didn't move away. He stared, and stared, and stared. I didn't know whether he was about to jump on me and scratch my face off. He stared. I stared. He breathed, I breathed.

All of a sudden, he jumped up and landed in my lap. I did not move. He walked in a circle for a bit, then plopped down on my thighs and curled into a tight, little ball. I wasn't sure what to do. Should I pet him? We'd never been intimate before, so I ran my hand over his back, without actually touching him. Then, as I spoke softly, I let my fingers lightly brush the top of his fur. And then, it happened. He started to purr. It was the most joyous sound I'd ever heard. Not because I'd won him over, but because I knew we would love each other forever.

We became inseparable. Somehow Alley knew when I was coming home and would wait silently at the door until I appeared. As soon as the door opened, he'd entwine himself around my ankles until I picked him up and kissed and hugged him. We ate together, slept together, he even stood guard at the bathroom door when I took a shower.

Unfortunately, in his eighth year of life, Alley was diagnosed with cancer and passed away. But I can honestly say, he was the love of my life. Unlike humans, I knew he would never hurt me, never intentionally leave me.

And yes, I did finally win Blondie's allegiance. Coni and I began seeing each other every weekend. Each time I entered the home, Blondie hid under the bed. I followed her and got down on the ground with her, constantly speaking to her in a gentle tone. Finally, after a few weeks, she knew she would never get rid of me; so, rather than being trapped under the bed with a human who never shut up, she picked the lesser of two evils and greeted me at the door. I was no longer a threat, no longer a stranger. Just a member of the family now.

ACCEPTANCE

I was ensconced in my new family: Coni, Blondie, and TJ. The bed was crowded, but the four of us made it work. And yes, I learned the technique for picking Blondie up and covering her anal glands with her tail. In fact, I came to love Blondie, anal glands and all.

My new family expanded when I finally met Coni's relatives: her father, a big, tough guy named Joe; Mary, her mother, a gentle soul; and her loving sister, Candace. Coni was not "out" to her family; but as was the case with many families back then, they suspected the "deviation." But if it was never stated out loud, no one was forced to deal with it.

Just as Nana had done when I first met her, Joe, Mary, and Candace embraced me as one of their own. I had finally found a place of belonging for myself. But this family had something special that mine did not: food. Coni's sister, mother, and Nana were each phenomenal in the kitchen...Are all Italians great cooks, I wondered....The only member of the family who wasn't great in the kitchen? You guessed it: Coni. I couldn't have fallen in love with her sister, or even Nana. No! I had to fall for Coni.

Coni's cooking was a small sacrifice to make as I now had a home for Thanksgiving, Christmas, New Year's, and birthday celebrations. My side though, my Jewish side, had nowhere to go. Once I went to a friend's house for a Passover Seder, but it was a painful experience for me, reminding me of everything I'd lost at an early age....

My father's youth had been tough. He was a scrappy kid in Brooklyn, trying his best to scrounge money to support his family. My mother nicknamed him "Fatty" hoping he'd put on weight. Although muscular, he had little meat on his bones. The food went to the younger siblings first. By the time I was born, my father had added weight, but I was shocked when I looked at his childhood pictures: an emaciated body, a sunken face.

Coni's dad was a big, strong bear of a man. He had started as a truck mechanic and eventually worked his way up to owning a gas station while saving some of his wages. This was Nana's son, the one whose father had died when he was six months old. Nana had struggled to support an infant by working sales in Macy's department store.

*

Truth is, everyone I knew grew up struggling in America. The first generation here, our grandparents; the second generation, our parents. Those of us in the third generation had opportunities that those before us did not; but still, we had to work hard to move forward. Remember, no medical care, no food stamps, no nothing for the earlier generations, just grit, and self-reliance, and determination.

And believe me, there was plenty of openly aggressive prejudice throughout society, especially prejudice against immigrants even though they took the lowest-paying, most repetitive jobs requiring the longest hours. Jobs that other people who were better off had rejected, but that those same people relied on to support their more privileged way of life.

When I was working at the drug detox hospital, I became friendly with one of the janitorial staff, a man named John. He invited me and my boyfriend, Steve (before Lainey) to a party in the housing project where he lived. Here we were, two whites in an all-Black housing project. Steve was a little nervous. I'd spent a large part of my childhood interacting with all kinds of people. My best friend through junior high school was African American, my closest friend through college was Puerto Rican....Am I trying to pat myself on the back for being unbiased? No. These interactions with people who weren't the same race I was, were just a normal part of my day. If I liked you, if you liked me, let's be friends. I loved being exposed to other cultures, food, religions, and unique ways of dressing.

John had recently married, and that day he was throwing a celebration for friends, family members, and other acquaintances who had not been invited to the wedding, which had been a small family affair. I was honored that John had invited us—and I wasn't going to miss the celebration simply because I felt anxious at being an outsider and not fitting in.

When Steve and I arrived at the party, the guests embraced us, made us feel welcome, and the party exploded with a demonstration of warmth, infectious laughter, and endless heartfelt embraces. I knew from stories I'd heard that if the celebration had been an all-white party and two Black guests had arrived, the reverse would not necessarily have been true. The prejudice would have been front and center. But here the opposite was the case. Later, I found the same warm welcome when I conducted home visits to patients with families that were different than myself.

I once attended a ceremony at a Black church where a friend received acknowledgment for the good work she had done in her community. The church service was followed by a luncheon. The singing...*wow*. It was like a free Broadway show. And people couldn't feed me enough food and treats. Everyone stopped by the table where I was sitting to welcome me into their place of worship. How tragic are the barriers we erect between ourselves and other people, based on what? A different way of speaking, a different religion, a different skin color? What a loss to the potential expansion of the human soul to not reach across these meaningless barriers and enrich each other's hearts and minds!

And you probably think that being a white girl, I didn't experience prejudice. But remember, I'm Jewish, and I look Jewish.

When my father was working, my mother told him we needed more money than he was bringing home. He applied for a job at a bank. My father stood in a long line outside the bank; the heat that day was sweltering. Some of the people in line almost fainted, or they couldn't take it and left. But my father stood for three hours in that heat to take a math test for the bank's accounting department. Afterwards, a bank manager called him into the interview room and told him, "You scored the highest score on the test today, but we don't hire Jews."

No anti-discrimination laws back then. My father's heat exhaustion gained him nothing.

My sister arrived at her new college dorm on the first day of school. She put her clothes away then went to the cafeteria for something to eat. When she returned, her clothes had been thrown all over the hallway and a hand-written sign had been pasted on the door to her dorm room. The sign had a big swastika accompanied by the words *Go home Jew.*

You'd think by the time I was growing up, being six years younger than my sister, things would be different. I was in upstate New York, about fourteen years old, when I went to a local diner to get a Coca-Cola. I sat at the counter, the man behind it was serving other customers, and I said, "I'll have a Coke, please."

No response. So I said again, "I'll have a Coke, please."

Still no response. Yet the man continued to serve everyone else who walked in after me. Then I thought, *I look younger than I am...Maybe he thinks I don't have the money to make the purchase.* So I put the coins on the counter.

"I'll have a Coke, please."

He looked at the money, then stared lethally into my eyes, then looked at my neck. *My neck?* Then, I got it. I was wearing a necklace with a Jewish star. I left the diner, knowing I would never win this battle.

Even in friendly territory, explicit stereotyping continued. When I worked at the probation department, an administrative assistant who I liked and who I was friendly with, came up to me one day and said:

"You're Jewish, aren't you?"

"Yes," I replied.

"I just bought this Lotto ticket, can I rub it against you for good luck?'

I was shocked, but responded, "Okay, but if you win, I get ten percent."

We laughed, but it hurt my feelings.

Not seeing past the externals can be hurtful at best, but as we've seen throughout history, it can sometimes be lethal as well.

THE KNOCK ON THE DOOR

Being with Coni on weekends meant having the opportunity to live in a private house, if only for two days a week. I'd never experienced the feeling of sitting in a backyard, watching different species of birds swoop down and peck in the grass for their early meal. Was that what inner peace was supposed to feel like?

As a single woman, Coni was accepted into her suburban life with a hello wave from neighbors, short, surface conversations at the supermarket, baskets delivered to each other on special occasions….Something about her attracted the neighborhood children to enthusiastically run over and tell her about the day's adventures. And then the change happened.

It was subtle at first. Then it became blatant. A mother pulled her son away from Coni at the store and told him not to talk to her again. The boy was perplexed but followed his mother's command. Coni and I suspected why the shift came about, but we had been so careful not to touch in public, not to kiss, not to show any signs of intimacy. But being conscious of our persona in public was not enough, I guess.

When I was a kid growing up in a neighborhood alongside many Holocaust survivors, I was always told *beware of the knock on the door.* Apparently, the Nazis would knock on the Jews' doors in the middle of the night, drag the families out of bed, and take them to the concentration camps. I never thought that phrase would have any meaning in modern day life until the inevitable happened: the knock on the door.

Coni opened the door to a neighbor from across the street. A cop from an adjacent town, dressed in full uniform, his badge glinting in the sunlight, holstered gun on his hip. Another cop—a cop we didn't recognize—stood by silently, a smirk on his face. The first cop looked from Coni to me and back again. We said nothing. Then, he spoke.

"Listen to what I'm about to say, because I'm only going to say it once. If you two dykes don't get the hell out of this neighborhood, I swear I will burn your house down with both you cunts sleeping in it."

One last glare and he and his buddy were gone. I don't know how long it took until Coni and I closed the door. We were motionless, watching the cop, our so-called neighbor, ride off in his patrol car.

Now what?

We talked about getting Coni's father, Joe, involved. Owning a gas station, he'd given donations to local politicians and had some influence with the police, who gassed up their patrol cars at his station and brought their mechanical problems there. They in turn watched over the station when it was closed, because a cash business was always a lure for the criminal element. But I pointed out: "Look, I know your father would do what he could to protect us, but first you'd have to come out to your family. And because we might get a cop in trouble, part of your father's customer base would be lost, and maybe his gas station trashed at night."

I knew from working with cops at the courts and the corrections officers in prison that if you make trouble for one of their own, they'll make trouble for you.

"We can't do that to him," I said. "And, do you think you'll be untouched?" I continued. "You have a clean driving record now. How long before you're pulled over, stopped, given tickets, harassed also?"

"I don't know. I can't think straight right now," Coni said, unable to process her world suddenly being turned upside down.

I knew I wasn't responsible, but if Coni had never met me, none of this would have been happening. I felt like shit.

Us "dykes," had invaded the neighborhood, and *they* needed to clean us out before we infected their kids with our sicko vibes.

Imagine finally being settled…then, in a minute, the ground is pulled out from under you. What choices did we have? We talked for hours, but unfortunately the only choice we had was to move. Would we be able to find a more liberal, less prejudiced neighborhood, or would the same script play out over and over again wherever we went? But who was there to back us up? No one. We were on our own, just as other lesbians like the ones in Manhattan who were gangraped near the Hudson River, and those who might be declared unfit mothers and had to flee to safe houses with their babies. We had no power, no justice, just invisible victims.

Finally, after weeks of worrying and searching, we found a split ranch home not too far from Coni's family. We moved in, nervous that we'd be subjected to the same harassment and prejudice we had encountered earlier.

Then, there it was again, the knock on the door.

We opened the front door to a man and woman a little younger than us, carrying a welcome basket filled with luscious treats and a lovely card.

Was the couple's warm greeting and the welcome basket a neighborhood ritual? Did they know they were extending their welcome to a lesbian couple? We found out later that the wife was a successful real estate lawyer in the neighborhood. She knew we were two older women living alone. She had figured it out.

We became friends with the couple's family and several other families in the neighborhood. No one seemed to care about our sexual orientation. And then, shortly after we had moved in, I was standing outside when a car screeched to a halt in front of the driveway. A man dressed in a suit and tie exited. What the hell did he want? Was he police, or FBI?

"Hi," the strange man said.

"Hi," I cautiously responded.

He introduced himself then said, "My boyfriend and I live on the next block."

Did he say "boyfriend"?'

"We're having a party Saturday night," he went on, "and we'd like you and your partner to come."

Was he for real?

"Thank you. We'd love to," I replied.

When Saturday night arrived, off we went, anxious to meet other same sex people like ourselves who lived in the neighborhood. At the party, gays and lesbians emerged from their hidden caves: teachers, doctors, waiters and waitresses, secretaries, everyone.

I always loved the fact that the same people who did not want us in their neighborhoods gladly accepted our taxes, our money at local businesses, let us take care of them in hospitals, sometimes saving their lives, teaching their children, cleaning their homes, and all the rest we did for them. If a lesbian cured cancer they'd take the cure. But would they ever let us live in peace?

WHAT WE DARE NOT SPEAK

One day when I was in my late twenties, I was sitting with a bunch of friends when someone suggested we go around the group and share our most vivid memory of childhood. Tales of family picnics, special vacations, birthday parties brought a sense of nostalgic joy to all of us. At least it did until it was my turn.

To this day I have no explanation for what happened. I was having a great time and so was everyone else until I blurted out, "Death and dying."

Talk about buzzkill. Of course everyone was supportive, and I made jokes about never being invited to get-togethers again, but I still couldn't believe that had slipped out so unconsciously. But honestly, death and dying are the predominant memories of my childhood. Sure, we had family events, small, local trips; but in between the normalcy, someone was always dying.

When my mother had her first cancer, I was an infant. Of course I don't remember any of this. What I do remember is seeing my mother undressed later in life, her ribs sticking out on her right side, the muscle from that area removed, the skin burnt with a reddish tint from radiation, and a right arm that could never reach higher than her shoulder. Surgery back then was brutal.

My father's sister had breast cancer that spread to her bones when she was in her thirties. My mother's sister was dead by her late twenties or early thirties…I only know of her from pictures. My father's youngest sister had breast cancer at forty years old, a male first cousin of mine had testicular cancer in his twenties, another male prostate cancer at forty, my father's older sister lung cancer, and my maternal grandfather came to live with us when I was about ten: he was dying from cancer that had spread to his liver. Little did I know that in a few short years I'd be seeing that jaundiced skin and those bony ribs, and that I'd be inhaling that rotting smell of death from my own mother as she lay dying. And to add to the family legacy, after my mother died, I ran into her first cousin while on a vacation and found out that two of her three children had succumbed to the family curse.

I knew the inevitability of my own fate, so I started seeing a breast cancer surgeon at the age of thirty. I told Dr. Marcus my family history. He didn't flinch, just listened. A year later, after we knew each other well, he asked if I would share my family history with some medical students. Of course I said yes, and then I knew my family medical history was more than just routine. Unfortunately, I had to add a younger cousin with a brain tumor to the list later on.

The first time Dr. Marcus examined me he said, "I can't prevent you from getting cancer."

"I know that," I replied.

"But if you do everything I say, I will find it as early as possible."

He took my situation personally, as if he was going to make sure I was not going to die on his watch.

And so began yearly mammograms, then a physical check of my breasts every few months. Each time a lump showed up, Dr. Marcus had to make a decision. I had very dense, cystic breasts—hard to read using the diagnostic tools available back then. Dr. Marcus declared each lump benign, but he would tell me I had to come back a month later to make sure the lump had disappeared.

On occasion, a needle biopsy was performed in his office. So far, all was clear. I made it into my forties. Maybe the curse would not fall upon me.

When I went for my annual mammography, the radiologist usually had patients remain in the waiting room after the imaging procedure was finished; then she would read the results and bring them into the office to give the patient the news. But not me. I had to go home and wait for a call once the office had closed for the day: the radiologist needed time to concentrate on my films and compare them with previous results.

One day, after my monthly exam, the phone rang again.

"Hi. Dr. Rowena here."

"Hi, Dr. Rowena," I said in return. "So what's the news today?"

"There's been a change," Dr. Rowena said. "Enough so that I'm sending your films to Dr. Marcus for him to evaluate."

"Do you think—"

"It's hard to tell. If it is, it's very early. Dr. Marcus will know what to do."

At that point, I knew before I spoke to Dr. Marcus that the inevitable had happened.

I underwent a biopsy in the hospital. Coni and I went to Dr. Marcus's office the following week to learn the results. I knew my time had come, but I wasn't expecting the curve ball he lobbed at my head.

"I'm recommending a double mastectomy," he said.

I was shocked. "But nothing showed up in the other breast on the mammography," I said.

"I took a large sample from your right breast, and even if the left is clear at the moment, it's only a matter of time."

I always knew I would have a mastectomy at some point, but remove both breasts? Prophylactic mastectomies were not common back then. Coni and I left the office, went back home to think, rest, research, and make a decision. I called my father's youngest sister, who developed breast cancer at age forty. She called her breast surgeon for an opinion. His response?

"She should have done it yesterday."

And so all the opinions were the same: my primary care doctor, my radiologist, a doctor Coni knew at her hospital, my aunt's doctor. It was unanimous.

In addition to undergoing the double mastectomy, tissue expanders would be placed inside my chest; the procedure would be performed by another surgeon. Eventually, over the course of several months, the expanders would stretch my skin out to make a new home for saline implants.

The night before the surgery, Coni and I performed a farewell ceremony for my breasts. Then, she drew me tightly to her and whispered words that helped me survive the coming ordeal.

"I can't wait until the surgery is over," she said. "Because the next time I hold you, our chests will be closer together, and I'll feel your heart beating even stronger next to mine."

If I had any doubts about her feelings of having a disfigured partner, they were canceled at that moment.

Between the double mastectomy, the removal of several lymph nodes underneath both of my arms, and the second surgery for the tissue expanders, I was under the knife (as they say) for a long time. Coni and my friend Joanna, who was now a nurse, stayed at the hospital the full day, making sure I received proper post-surgical care. All my friends rallied around me: they visited me, they called me, they sent cards, they sent flowers, and I did bounce back pretty quickly.

Unfortunately, both saline implants caused problems for me. One deflated, the other caused me terrible pain. The surgeon offered to replace them, but I did not want to live my life in hospitals and doctors' offices, so I refused. I wanted my freedom back. My freedom from the family curse. So I had the surgeon remove both implants.

Coni and I went to a mastectomy store to buy a bra with molded replacements for my missing breasts. One of the bras we found looked good, but I decided the false breasts were too cumbersome for me. Coni then found other bras she felt she could reconfigure by placing soft material inside to mimic breasts. I still wear those bras to this day.

It took months physically and psychologically for me to attain a new and natural equilibrium…Could I ever wear this blouse again? Was this sweater too tight?

I can only imagine how difficult it is for those who lose an arm or a leg, having to relearn to walk or hold a glass, others watching them fully aware of the change. I was lucky that I was able to cover up my amputations; after a while, I became less self-conscious. Because of my radical choice back then, I outlived most of my relatives and made it to my fiftieth birthday.

It was now time to celebrate!

I MADE IT!

There was a small, lovely, Italian restaurant in Manhattan with great food. Yes, I know, Italian food again, but hey, it's my birthday, right? Of course I booked the place for a weekend luncheon. I invited only friends who'd lived with me through my ordeal to join Coni and me in celebration.

Sharon and her friend, Cathy, came in from Boston for the event, and of course my lovely older sister Sarah, who looked out for me during childhood, flew in from California where she was now living. My sister had remained my best friend throughout the years.

When I unexpectedly wound up as a lesbian, Sarah was the first person I called to share my news. I knew she would be accepting, because she'd always loved me unconditionally. And she'd spent a part of her life in New York around theater people, many of whom were gay and out, at least within the creative community.

My sister's theater journey began at an off-off-Broadway theater company in Brooklyn, where she worked with the theater's producer. Some of the actors who started there became big-time Broadway and film actors. Best of all, I was able to see all of their shows for free. What a treat.

Once when a young actor was just starting out, Sarah told me, "He's going to be big. He's so talented and so nice."

Boy was she right. They became good friends over the years; every time he appeared on Broadway, we were treated to free tickets and got to go backstage to say hello.

Sarah worked with a Broadway producer in Manhattan for a while then moved to Los Angeles, where she started her career as a script reader for a film producer. Then she worked in casting before finally winding up with a successful TV producer who had several hit series to her credit.

Sarah had done it. She'd followed her dream and turned her fantasies into reality. I missed her terribly after she moved to the West coast, but she still protected me even from afar.

The big event each year when she still lived in New York was her fabulous Oscar party, which she held in her apartment. It was mobbed: actors, directors, writers, chorus folk, lots of food, and, best of all, backstage gossip about well-known stars—the divas, the bastards, the bitches, and the good ones who were kind and respectful to all regardless of their role on the project.

The gossiping continued when she moved to Hollywood. For example, one female TV star berated everyone and forced staff to have to choose lots to decide who would be the latest victim when she demanded someone come on set. And then, there was the handsome talented actor from a hit TV series that filmed near my sister's studio. He and his buddies played basketball during their downtime. Every time my sister passed by on the way to work, the actor would stop, turn around, give her that smile women still faint from to this day and say, "Hi, Sarah. How are you doing?"

Sometimes he complimented her on her clothes, or how her TV show was going. Apparently, no matter how well-known he became as he and his movies achieved international recognition, he remained respectful and caring to all. My definition of a mensch.

When the cancer in my breasts attacked me, Sarah wanted to fly in and help. I had plenty of good friends in addition to Coni to help me, and I didn't want Sarah to have to relive our family nightmare. So I told her not to come. Just this once, at least, I could protect her.

*

When Sarah flew in from California for my fiftieth birthday party, she stayed at a hotel. I loved room service, and we ordered and ordered over and over again until I think the server wanted to move in with us just to get some sleep.

Sarah gave me a lovely pair of earrings; but most of all, she gave me a big, all-encompassing hug, along with a look of big sister pride on her face.

What a crazy, wild birthday celebration. Delicious food, a skit about me performed by Sharon and her friend Cathy from Boston. And then, music, and dance. I think the restaurant was shocked when we pushed back the tables and turned the place into a dance hall. It became so infectious that the waiters, house staff, and kitchen employees joined us on the dance floor. At one point we even had a conga line that shimmied its way outside onto the sidewalk. Someone brought a leather-covered book, a kind of a diary or journal, which everyone signed, and in which everyone wrote a little something about my friendship with them.

Externally, I might have lost my breasts, but internally, I could barely contain all the love, affection, and acceptance from the extraordinary group of human beings I had alongside me.

The party ended on a high note. Coni waited a day or two before sharing her bad news with me.

"I think something is wrong with your sister."

I stared at her. "What do you mean?"

"Sarah has a really dry cough."

"So what?" I said. "She'll get over it."

"It's not a normal cough."

Remember, Coni had been working in hospitals all of her adult life. She also had my mental health instincts: she possessed a built-in alarm buzzer that detected physical illness.

I called my sister the next day. As she spoke, I heard the cough over and over again. I was so distracted at the party, I hadn't noticed it.

"Sarah," I said, "what's with the cough?"

"It's nothing."

"Did you see a doctor?"

"Yes, it's allergies."

I shared the news with Coni.

"That's not an allergy-related cough. She needs to see a pulmonologist."

Next phone call.

"Sarah, Coni thinks you need to see a lung doctor and at least get an X-ray of your chest."

"It's okay," my sister insisted. "I saw another doctor. It's my thyroid."

Her thyroid? Back to Coni.

"It's not thyroid. Make her go to the pulmonologist and get a scan."

But before I could pressure my sister again, her best friend Diane called me.

"Your sister collapsed and is in the emergency room. I'll call when we have news."

Oh, God, please, I prayed to myself. *I'm begging you. Don't do this. Not to Sarah. Not to my sweet, loving sister Sarah.*

Then the call.

"Sarah has lung cancer," Diane said.

Part of me wanted to scream at my sister, *Why didn't you go to the doctor when I first talked to you?* But of course, I never said that to her.

Then I looked back over the diary my friends had written in during my birthday party and noticed something peculiar from my sister. Everyone else had put tidbits about my relationship with them in the book, fun times we'd had together, their love for me. But my sister's words, I realized, were weird. It's as if she'd written a checklist, not about childhood incidents we shared or the friendship we'd sustained over the years, but a list of items proving I was okay with my life. How happy she was that I had a loving relationship with Coni, who she knew would always take care of me. How wonderful to be surrounded with good friends and have a job I liked. It was a list confirming that I had other people nearby to care for me. Because as I looked back, I realized that at my party, my sister already knew she was terminally ill. All her treatments had failed, even though I was to know nothing about her nightmare until later, after my party. She was still my older sister protecting me as she'd always done.

I was not going to let my sister die. No matter what I had to do, I was not going to lose Sarah. Fortunately, Coni heard about a promising new cancer drug that had been tested successfully in mice. It had been approved for the next stage of trials in humans who were deemed terminally ill. The only problem? The upcoming trial would be a small study involving a limited number of patients, and the injections had to be administered once a month on the East Coast. That meant Sarah flying in from California. Would she be able to handle it?

"Yes, yes," I assured the nurse who was helping to evaluate which patients would be chosen for the study. I called the nurse almost every day, pleading with her to accept my sister into the study. I explained my family's cancer history, how I'd lost most of my relatives including my mother when I was young, I *begged* the nurse to help my sister. After several weeks, the nurse told me the committee would make its decision over the weekend, and she would call me on Monday at one o'clock in the afternoon to let me know whether my sister was on the roster.

Can you imagine what that weekend was like? I hardly slept, hardly ate, couldn't concentrate on anything. At precisely one o'clock, Monday afternoon, the phone rang.

"Yes?" I said hardly able to breathe.

"Your sister is accepted into the clinical trial," the nurse said.

"Oh, thank you, thank you, thank you!"

After the phone call, I thought I would collapse. But there was too much to do.

On my sister's first trip to New York for the study, we stayed at a hotel near the hospital in case she developed a bad reaction as a result of the injection. But the reaction before the medicine was administered was worse.

Sarah had lost weight, the coughing had increased, she could hardly talk through her breathing difficulties. To add to the misery, she kept vomiting every time she ate....She was fading fast, flying to the East Coast for every appointment. Was I torturing her by urging her to participate in the trial? Was she doing it for herself...or to placate me?

Finally the trial ended, and so did my hope. The drug did not work.

✶

I called my sister every day, sometimes she could speak, other times the breathing difficulty overwhelmed her words. It was early fall, and I made plans to see her over Thanksgiving. Not too long afterwards, Sarah entered a hospice. Her birthday was a few weeks later, and her friends threw her a party at the hospice and included me via my phone.

At the same time that my sister was in hospice care, Coni's father was also ill. He had been admitted to a hospital on the East Coast with complications of diabetes.

Around this time, Diane, my sister's friend called. "Sarah has taken a turn for the worst," she told me. "You need to get here right away."

I was a fearful flyer, but Coni couldn't accompany me, as her father remained in critical condition. How was I going to be able to get on a plane by myself? But I had no choice. Sarah would never have abandoned me. I was about to embark on the most terrifying experience of my life: traveling alone on a plane to say goodbye to my dying sister.

A friend gave me a couple of Ambien, and as I entered the plane, I told the flight attendant that I was a fearful flyer and was going to knock myself out with drugs. Would she please make sure I was awake after we landed?

The pills worked. I don't remember anything more than getting off the plane to find Diane waiting for me by baggage claim. She helped me roll my luggage to the parking area; then I climbed into the passenger seat of her car. Before I could breathe a sigh of relief that I'd braved the plane ride, Diane said, "I'm sorry, but Sarah died while you were in the air. I'm taking you to the hospice. They promised to hold her body so you could have a chance to say goodbye to her."

No! No!

My sister, my best friend, the most caring, loving person I had ever met in my life, was dead. It couldn't be. It just couldn't be.

I cried the entire drive to the hospice. I felt bad for Diane, for she was grieving too, and there was no way she could possibly have comforted me.

*

The hospice was housed on a beautiful piece of land surrounded by greenery and woodlands. An aide took me to Sarah's room and left me alone with her. I pulled a chair up beside my sister's bed to speak to her; I took her left hand in mine. Her hand was still warm. Even though Sarah wasn't breathing, perhaps she knew I was there. I looked over at her right arm and saw that it was swollen to three times the size of her left arm. How much had she suffered?

I glanced out of the window beside her bed. A robin with a rust-colored chest strutted around the lawn. A cardinal perched high in a tree called to his mate. As I raised my head, smidgens of white tufted clouds glided across a blue and white sky.

Outside, nature at its best; inside nature at its worst: only a thin pane of glass between them. I looked down at my sister's mangled body, her hand now cold. Sarah was dead.

I returned home, hoping Sarah was now at peace, knowing I never would be. Could I have done more for her? Could I have prevented her death? Although in my mind I knew the answer to be no in both cases, a mind cannot control a grieving heart.

ONLY THE GOOD DIE YOUNG

By now I was the assistant head of the counseling department at the outpatient methadone clinic. A small raise came with the title—and a large amount of responsibility. Not only did I counsel patients individually and supervise other team members, but I also had to handle any crisis in the clinic when my boss was not there. The clinic was the place where Michael, during a counseling session, held a knife to my throat. In addition to individual counseling, I ran a couple of groups: one for those with mixed addictions (usually alcohol and heroin) and a separate women's group, where we worked on resumes and role-played job interviews.

MELISSA

Melissa had been in the job-seeking group and had successfully transitioned into employment. I'd been counseling her individually for over a year. Her evolution was amazing.

To hear Melissa speak, she had the life she had always dreamed of. She worked in sales at a high-end boutique, and she had private customers who paid her to dress them for special events. She'd been clean for over a year, had a nice apartment in midtown, friends of the nonaddicted variety, and a boyfriend who had recently moved in with her. Having access to designer clothes, she was always impeccably dressed, as opposed to myself, who schlepped around in jeans, a blouse, and running shoes in case an emergency arose.

For several weeks, Melissa regaled me with tales of dining out with her boyfriend and exclusive parties they attended. She even brought in pictures of the new living room furniture she'd just purchased. I was happy for her, but her need to constantly tell me about all of the wonderful things in her life began to feel like a coverup. I was more interested in what she wasn't telling me.

On one particular day, Melissa arrived at her counseling session on time (as usual), clothes beautiful, hair and makeup perfect, her smile not quite what I was used to. I usually wait until a patient is ready to talk about an underlying difficult situation, but this time my instincts told me "time's up." So I interrupted her itemized perfection.

"Melissa, enough with the diversionary tactics. I feel like you're playing me."

So much for a soft method to ease behind her wall of defense. But I had to put an end to the hide-and-seek routine.

"I'm not playing you," she replied. "Everything I told you is true."

"I don't doubt that. But I want to hear about what you're not telling me."

"Why are you even asking me this?" she said.

"You know, I've seen you at your worst: stinking from the streets, shaggy, unkempt, living from one drug high to the next. You bared your soul to me as I watched you transition from the streets back into a constructive life and genuine happiness. You have my utmost respect, but now I need your respect. I know something is eating away at you, I see the stress in your eyes. So please, let's not play games. We've worked together too long."

Unaware, she turned away from me.

"You can't even look at me," I said.

"It's nothing," she replied.

"I know you well enough to know it's not nothing."

"Okay," she finally admitted, "my boyfriend cheated on me."

A crisis perhaps, but not a disaster. I kept pushing.

"Tell me about the cheating."

"That's it."

"No feelings, no thoughts about it?"

Silence. I watched as she grappled with conflicted impulses. Should she open up? Should she stay shut down? One last push.

"Are you using again?"

"No. No, I'm not…My boyfriend, Dereck…"

"What about Dereck?"

She turned away so abruptly, I thought she would fall off the chair. Then, the tears flowed.

"I can't. I can't talk about it. I can't."

"Please turn back and look at me. You know this office is the safest space in the world."

"No, I can't. You'll hate me."

"Not possible."

"Yes, you will."

Oh, boy. Victimology thinking. Now she had me really worried.

"Is Dereck hurting you?"

She snapped her head back around as if someone had betrayed her.

"How did you know?"

"Because I've dealt with this many times before."

"You have?"

I nodded my head yes, confirming that I knew all about it.

"When did it start?" I asked her.

A huge sigh followed as Melissa got herself together. "Shortly after he moved in. He kept complaining about little things that I did that annoyed him. Then, he started making demands."

"Like what?"

"Like he expected me home at a certain time. Like I was a child with a curfew. It only got worse from there. One time…one time he actually banged my head into the wall until I passed out."

She burst into hysterics. Truthfully, I wanted to cry myself. She was so frightened, so alone. I knew she was in real danger. On top of that, she reeked from her own sense of failure. In her mind, she'd come so far then had thrown it all away.

Apparently, Dereck's control over her had continued to escalate. He took charge of the money, buying the groceries, demanding more of Melissa's attention, slapping her if he didn't like answers to his questions.

"Last week, he wanted me to go out with his friends for dinner," Melissa told me. "I said no. I had had a long day at work, one of the other sales associates had called in sick. I just wanted to sleep."

She looked to the other side of the room as if watching a replay of the incident in her mind.

"He got angry and pushed me against the dresser. He was completely out of control. He started choking me. Said he wanted to go out and I was coming with him. I thought he would kill me."

She removed her scarf to reveal the bruising around her neck.

"I tried to get the real Dereck back by putting on music, dancing with him, which he always loves. For a moment, he'd seem like himself, then something would set him off. Two days ago, he said he could easily kill me if he wanted to. He grabbed a kitchen knife and held it near my chest."

This was worse than I had imagined.

"Have you told anyone else about this?"

"I can't," she said. "If he finds out, things will be worse. Maybe he will kill me. How could I have let this happen? I've worked so hard to get my life together and then in a second, I destroy the whole thing."

"It's not destroyed. Everything you've accomplished is still there. We just need to get you your power back."

Melissa's father had died when she was quite young. Her mother entered into a deep depression, fell apart, and could never put all of the pieces back together again. Although emotionally and psychologically crippled, she still took care of Melissa as best she could.

I understood the lure a man like Dereck held for Melissa. Someone who presented himself as strong, in control, a savior to someone whose childhood had been so unsafe. And maybe some of the qualities he presented would have been great if he was also a decent human being. But this man was a phony, a fake, a user, drawing Melissa in with breadcrumbs he sprinkled along her path. And now he was volatile and dangerous.

The escalation of his physical abuse scared me a lot. But I also knew Melissa was in a state of paralysis: fearful of retribution if she told him to leave, and fearful of facing her own neediness that made her vulnerable to him in the first place.

"Don't tell me to dump him. I know I should, but I'm scared."

"Do you think he might actually kill you?"

"Yes, yes, I do."

"I want you to listen to me," I said. "Unfortunately this is more common than most people know."

I've seen very well-to-do women who were abused at home but had to remain quiet, because if they conveyed even a hint of domestic violence to their circle of friends it might result in their husband losing clients, or even his career. And after all he was the breadwinner.

"Okay, I know an organization with groups and counselors for battered women," I told Melissa. "They're supportive, nonjudgmental, and won't push you out of your comfort zone. They're highly experienced and will take you through every step along the way, and of course I'll be here too. I can make you an appointment for an intake interview."

"But, Dereck watches my every move…Where will I tell him I'm going?"

"They'll set it up at your convenience. Maybe a lunch hour, maybe you'll say you're working late and they'll see you then. They know how to do this."

"I don't know," Melissa said.

"It can't hurt just to meet them. If you're not convinced, then you don't have to go back. You've got nothing to lose."

"And you've sent others there?"

"Yes, with great success."

I set her up with one of the counselors I'd worked with before. Melissa liked having other women to talk to who were going through the same issues—especially women who'd come out the other side. Every week I counseled Melissa. With her permission, I also spoke to the counselor at the women's group. She was making great progress.

When the time finally came to kick Dereck out, Melissa obtained an order of protection, and had her male cousin Conrad at her apartment when Dereck took away his possessions and left her life. She changed the locks, notified her neighbors and building staff in case Dereck came back. The court order stated he was forbidden to enter the premises. Then, she told her boss at work. It took several weeks before Melissa felt safe. She continued with the women's group and her counseling with me. It had been a month, and no sign of Dereck.

"Maybe he's moved on to someone else," she told me at that point, a touch of regret over the loss of the fantasy she'd once engaged in.

About two months later, Melissa missed her appointment with me. I called the women's group. No, she'd missed her appointment there too. I was a wreck. I knew before the call came in that disaster was looming. A neighbor, who had heard fighting next door, called the cops for a wellness check. Dereck had somehow entered the building, crashed through the apartment door, beat Melissa, then threw her out of her fifteenth-story apartment window, her body splattered in an alley below.

I was devastated. Traumatized. Melissa was a wonderful person, and I admired her. The strength it took to turn her life around was stunning: leaving the streets, overcoming her drug addiction, her bravery to take action and kick Dereck out. I did not know whether I would have had the ability to accomplish all that she had.

I wound up back in therapy. Everyone in my profession needs help on and off. Sometimes its peer counseling, other times private counseling to get through the traumas we witness. As much knowledge as we have, as skilled as we are, we're still human.

I had one therapist friend who had lost a patient to suicide. It took him months of going over every detail, discussing the suicide with colleagues, looking for the place he might have made a mistake. Nothing showed up, but still the scars remained.

I went through the same process. I knew I had no control over Dereck, and that the women's group had done everything it could emotionally, psychologically, and legally to help Melissa. But the loss of a patient, especially one who'd worked so hard and come so far, would never quite go away. Not even to this day, years later.

Whenever I hear the line "only the good die young" from the Billy Joel song, I think of Melissa and my mother. Does that line really tell the truth? Or is it a lie we tell ourselves whenever reality seems so unfair? I have had to confront this question over and over again in my own life.

A CLOUD OF DOUBT

I had been experiencing these doubts over the course of my career, but had I ever actually helped anyone? My work was difficult to evaluate, unlike that of a surgeon who repairs someone's heart, the operation is successful, the patient goes back to his improved life. Job done! Or an eye doctor who removes a cataract and restores someone's sight. Voilà! Or a business person who looks at the balance sheet and admires new profits each quarter. Success! Or a teacher who notes all of the students' improved grade scores at the end of the year. Good job!

What about professions like mine where patients come and go all of the time? If a clinical social worker has a successful run with a patient, does the patient's improved life continue after the professional relationship with them ends? I continue to see people during times of crisis. Do they backslide? What has my life's work meant?

I had experienced these feelings at times during the course of my career, but the deaths of Melissa and my sister exacerbated my doubts, and I couldn't shake the feelings.

Maybe it was time to leave my job as a counselor, sit in a safe office behind a desk typing away at an inanimate computer that could always be fixed if it died—or else a new one would arrive the next day without fanfare. Although I put on a good external show, I felt shredded from the inside out.

DEZ

About a month after Melissa's death, I received a call from a former colleague with whom I'd worked at the inpatient detox hospital. We had fun catching up; then she told me that a former patient of mine, Dez, was looking for me. She did not provide him with any information regarding my whereabouts, of course; so he said to her, "Tell her I'll be in the park near the hospital on Saturday at 11 A.M. I hope she'll meet me there."

The colleague and I spent a good half hour trying to decide what Dez could possibly want after all these years. Would he add to my growing list of doubts about my skills by berating me for failing him?

Dez was a smart guy, finished college, then threw his future away on gambling. His addiction to gambling was Drug #1. Next came cocaine snorted in the morning so he would be alert at the casino tables. Finally, he used heroin at night for sleep. He first administered the narcotic by snorting, then moved on to skin popping, then finally mainlining. He was a mess. But don't tell Dez that. According to him, he was the smartest person in the world, and maybe on some level he was. He'd learned to use our hospital to his advantage. He'd come into detox for thirty days, be discharged, spend the required amount of time outside the hospital so he would be eligible for readmission, then return for another detox. Three full years of the same pattern. Yet he was always cooperative with all, never a problem.

I liked Dez. Even though he had a higher educational level than most of the other patients, he was never condescending and happily participated in all activities. He also became my teacher. No, not in the way you think. Every time he returned, he assessed my newly developed skills. Here are some examples of his evaluations: "You seem so much more relaxed than the last time I was here."… "You know, the guys really respect you."…"You handled that asshole well. He needed someone to set him straight."

But who would set Dez straight? Nothing I did worked. His revolving-door treatment felt endless, until one day his superior mental faculties failed him.

Casinos began noticing that Dez was card counting; he was banned from each gambling mecca, one by one. Now what? *Hmm. How about a jewelry heist? Get the gems, sell them on the black market, make a fortune. Perfect.*

There is one big problem with impulsive crimes. You get caught. Successful heists take months, even years of planning, but Dez was on top of this. Literally.

Dez entered the store he'd targeted in the middle of the night from the roof. Too bad he hadn't assessed the roof as carefully as he had assessed my evolving skills. Part of the roof gave way, and Dez found himself stuck holding on to a pipe until the police came to save him in the morning. Trial, conviction, upstate prison with extra time tacked on for drug possession. Failure for Dez, failure for me.

On his last visit to our facility, detoxing to prepare for jail, he was scared out of his mind and shocked that a man who once stood above all others was now about to fall off his perch and drop down into the dirt below. I felt bad for him.

I often held small group sessions for patients facing jail time, so they could meet other people who'd been inside themselves. No one ever refused to help another person during these prison orientation groups. The volunteers shared their insights, advice, and mistakes. I hadn't yet started working in the criminal justice system, so I got schooled as well. Some of the advice:

"Be respectful of the corrections officers, do what they tell you to do. Once they get to know you and trust you, you'll have a little more freedom and privileges."

"You see someone getting in the face of others, stay away from them. They'll take you down with them."

"They toss the cells for contraband when you least expect it. If you have shit in your cell, make sure you hide it where they don't look. Behind a wall might be good." (I'm not sure how constructive that particular piece of advice was.)

Then, from an older guy: "Someone will try to be your friend. Watch your back until you know the guy's for real. Otherwise you'll get used, maybe set up to take the fall for something you didn't do."

Then, I chimed in. "Try to do something constructive while inside."

Back to the patients.

"Yeah, man. Read, learn, stay in touch with family and make a better life when you get out."

How ironic that this advice came from a patient who had been paroled and was now back inside a detox facility.

Dez's last day with us was rough. It wasn't just his fear; his perception of himself had crash-landed, causing major injuries to his psyche and self-image. My final words to him: "Do something inside that gets you in touch with who you really are as a person, the one before the drug use. And if you can help others while inside, it's the best natural high there is."

It had been well over a decade since I'd seen Dez. Now what should I do?

If he was back on his high horse and was contacting me so he could criticize what I did for him, I was in no shape to handle the meeting. At the same time, I felt I had to suck it up no matter what was awaiting me. As you know, I'd never abandoned a patient.

I entered the park at the appointed time, and a man who looked familiar called my name. Was this Dez? The man was dressed in pressed slacks, expensive-looking shoes, his hair molded in an obviously costly cut, his eyes shining with self-satisfaction. It was Dez. I took a deep breath. Was I about to hear, *Hey, look what I did on my own without your lousy help?*

"Hi, Dez," I greeted him. "You're looking well."

Dez replied, "I feel great."

A pause. Still no clue as to motive.

"Can I get you some coffee or something?" he asked. There was a kiosk nearby selling coffee and treats. Still no clue.

"No, thank you," I said.

"Here, sit, relax, I want to talk to you."

I sat down on the bench next to him.

"I thought you might want to know what happened to me since I was scared shitless when I went upstate."

"I'm sure you were," I said.

"But that little group you held," he replied, "you know...that prison orientation one. It helped me a lot."

"That's good to hear," I said.

"The last time I saw you was my last day on drugs," Dez said.

"That's great, Dez," I replied. "Really great."

"And what you said that day stuck with me."

I had no idea what I had said that day, it was so long ago.

Dez reminded me.

"You said, the decisions you make from here on out define your future—and, most of all, who you are as a person."

I said that? But it *sounded* like something I would have said.

"Even though I was fucked up and had no faith in myself, you still had faith in me that I could change," Dez said. "So I wanted to tell you what happened while I was in prison."

"All right," I replied.

Then Dez began: "The tips the guys gave me in the detox group really helped. I respected the COs, did what they told me, stayed away from the troublemakers. I remembered you saying that helping others could be a natural high. With the corrections officer's okay and the warden's approval, I started a group to teach reading to those with little education."

"Wow," I said with genuine admiration, "that's impressive."

"I helped others with their court cases, reading legal documents and helping them do research."

He stopped and looked over at me for more approval, so I gave him a smile of pride. Not for my work with him, but for his work on himself.

"Then, when I got out," Dez continued, "I took some adult learning courses in law and sociology. You know, basic stuff."

"Are you a lawyer?"

"No. No," he replied. "I'm a paraprofessional at a law firm. I work with others facing jail time, and I help drug users. The clients trust me, open up to me. I have insights the lawyers don't have because I lived that life."

Was this the same Dez I saw for three years in a revolving-treatment process without end?

He continued: "I had a former law firm client come back recently to thank me for my help, and something else you said stuck with me."

"What was that?"

"You told me that whatever I got out of our sessions together belonged to me, not to you, and I should take it with me and pass it on to others. So when this client came back to thank me, I realized I had never thanked you. So that's why I wanted to meet. So, thank you."

My eyes welled with tears...I was particularly vulnerable after my sister's death and Melissa's murder. I was afraid my professional facade would break, and I'd start blubbering like a two-year-old. A tear dripped down my cheek. I looked over at Dez, and he too had tears in his eyes. Always prepared for tears, I handed him a tissue and took one for myself. Then the two of us cracked up laughing, knowing how ridiculous we must look to other people passing by.

We said our goodbyes, and Dez left.

I was reminded how, in my profession, despite the strength and confidence we project to other people—be they colleagues, friends, family—we too occasionally need validation. Dez had given me that gift.

THE UNIMAGINABLE

After Sarah and Melissa's death, I was finally able to return to the secure routines of work and my home life with Coni. My emotional losses had been easing off a little at a time.

Then I got a call from Bev, our matchmaking friend who had held the New Year's Day parties where I first met Coni. Meryl, the woman Lainey had left me for, had died from a respiratory problem. I think I sent a condolence note, but honestly I can't remember, because shortly thereafter terrorists flew two planes into the Twin Towers and life as we knew it in New York changed in a microsecond.

I had kept my apartment in Manhattan, as it was near my job. I often worked late and slept overnight in the apartment. After the terrorist attack, my phones, internet, and TV all went offline. The only means I had of keeping informed of the evolving situation was a radio. I had no way to get in touch with Coni, friends, or relatives.

Communications eventually came back on-line, and I notified everyone I knew that I was all right. I watched the replays on TV, seeing people run from the towers covered in debris, looking for shelter and safety. Never did I expect that one of those people was Lainey.

The next morning Bev called and told me that Lainey was in the second tower but had made it out alive. At what cost to herself and her colleagues, I wondered?

When I awoke a day later, I looked outside my window, and saw dozens of army-type vehicles filled with soldiers armed with an assortment of weapons. The street outside was a two-way street, but all traffic had stopped, only the soldiers were visible. At some point, I went downstairs and was greeted with two situations I was not prepared for.

First, there I was in midtown Manhattan surrounded not just by soldiers on every corner, but with total, deadly silence. The lack of noise was disorienting. This was Manhattan, the noise capital of the world. But worse than the sense that my hearing had suddenly gone was the visual overload of depressed, frightened people handing out flyers with pictures of loved ones and tabs on the bottom listing contact information. In whispered voices I heard: *Have you seen my daughter? My husband? My wife? My son?* On and on and on. I don't know how many scores of people were roaming the streets looking for information on loved ones....

A sheltered bus stop with clear plastic protection from the rain stood on the street opposite my window. I walked over and looked at the now opaque walls lined with over a hundred flyers of missing persons. As I walked down the block to buy groceries, a soldier checked my ID at every corner. A day or two later, as travel on the streets of Manhattan began to resume, Coni and I decided I should return to our home.

I made my way over to Grand Central Station to catch a train home. It too was lined with soldiers and encased in an eerie silence. I found my way to my train and sat down. Within seconds, a group of soldiers came running down to the platform, screaming, "Everyone out now! Run, run, upstairs, *now!*"

We ran for our lives, rushing into the main lobby, where a gauntlet of soldiers had created a lane for us to run through in order to get out onto the street. Apparently, a bomb threat had been called in to the station. I was exhausted from fear, anxiety, and stress. I decided to walk back to my apartment.

I thought about Lainey. I couldn't imagine what she was going through, first having lost Meryl and then being inside the Twin Towers during the terrorist attack. Bev had told me that Lainey did not want to talk about what had happened. I could understand that and I could respect that.

But after all that had gone on, I knew I needed to get in touch with her soon. Even though our relationship had ended badly, it was time to resurrect the friendship. When Bev gave me the okay a few months later, I called Lainey. We agreed to meet at a local coffee shop.

When I arrived at the restaurant, I walked right past her. She called my name, getting my attention. I slipped into the booth opposite her, wondering how, after all that had happened, we would begin a conversation. Not only had we broken up, but Lainey's recent double whammy—the Twin Towers collapsing, and Meryl's death—loomed quietly over us.

She smiled at me, I smiled at her. But I realized almost immediately that a special light was missing in her eyes. That spark of hope and fearless adventure that had always drawn other people to her was gone. Would it return?

We ordered our food and got past the awkward part by talking gossip relating to anyone we had known during our time together. I realized there was a bond between us that would never be broken. It wasn't sexual, it was based upon a time when our innocence had still basically been intact; we were young with hopes and dreams driving us forward, each day a new adventure, ripe fantasies pervading our futures. But that time had long since passed; still, we could relive it together through the memories we shared of those moments and the feelings we had experienced.

Our renewed friendship began with activities that we both enjoyed: long walks around the city, where Lainey, a New York City history buff and a fan of the city's architecture, pointed out various architectural styles and building facades, detailing their historical significance. Here I was a native New Yorker, and Lainey—not a native by any stretch—knew more about my home city than I did. She loved art museums, dance recitals, and especially theater.

Unlike other people I knew, Lainey was as enthusiastic about off- and off-off-Broadway shows as she was about what New Yorkers call the tourist shows. Emerging writers, actors, directors, learned their craft on the fringes of Broadway. So when I took her to a small, black box theater I'd been to before, I knew she'd enjoy the experience. The audience was seated around three sides of the stage.

As we took our seats, I noticed Lainey tensing up. Then she started looking around with nervous eyes.

"Are you okay?" I asked.

"Hmm…how do we get out of here if something happens?" Lainey replied.

I knew the small, confined space of the theater, had drawn her mind back to the experience of the Twin Towers.

"You see over there?" I said. "That's where the actors come in, and behind that is a dressing room and hallway that leads back to the main lobby where we came off the elevator. There are also stairs we can take down and avoid the elevator rush."

Lainey nodded. Then she seemed to enjoy the show. When we left, I said, "Let's take the stairs, it's faster," hoping to reassure her we would reach the street outside—and safety—soon.

When we hit the sidewalk, I heard a big sigh of relief from Lainey. I saw her smile as she looked up at the open sky.

Our friendship continued after that day at the theater, and I liked having a "city" friend who enjoyed all the action and hyper stimulation as much as I did. When the show *Come From Away* opened, it got rave reviews. Here was a hybrid drama and musical about passengers stranded in flight in a small community up north after the airspace was closed following the 9/11 attacks. The community takes in the diverse group of passengers, welcoming them as their own and ensuring them a safe space to recover from their hellish nightmare. I asked Lainey if she'd like to see the show, and she enthusiastically said yes, knowing the subject matter full well.

As we sat in our seats watching the lovely show about strangers coming together to help others, I found I had tears in my eyes, as did most of the audience, especially the New Yorkers who had lived through the horror, each one of us having our own nightmarish memory. Everyone knew someone who had been in the towers, or they knew somebody who knew someone. One of Coni's colleagues at work had been pregnant with her first child and lost her husband in the tower collapse. An old friend of my sister's lived near the towers and developed severe respiratory issues; and there in the theater I of course was sitting next to someone who had lived through it and survived.

When a Broadway show ends, the lights go on and the actors come out for the applause and the acknowledgment from the crowd. The day Lainey and I saw *Come From Away,* a woman and her daughter who were sitting in the row in front of us got up as soon as the lights came up and started to leave. Something snapped in me. Maybe I was feeling protective of Lainey, or maybe my own memories of the horror got the best of me, but I yelled at the woman. "What the hell is wrong with you?" I said. "You disrespect the actors who just worked their asses off to give you a great show, and what about all of us who lived through 9/11, you disrespect us too and leave before the actors even take their bows?"

I knew I was off-the-wall, but the performance we had just watched was not merely a tourist show, it was real life for us. The woman looked at me like I was nuts, and maybe she was right. Then she and her daughter left anyway.

Lainey said nothing as we left the theater and headed to a restaurant for dinner. We were shown to a table, we smiled politely at the waitress, perused the menu, ordered our food, and watched the crowds of people rushing by the window, talking animatedly, laughing, and making the most of their leisure time.

Lainey sipped a glass of red wine. Then she suddenly said, "They said there was an accident. That a plane had crashed into the first tower, and it would be best if we left the building via the stairs. Some of us did, others did not."

She turned from the window and looked at me, not just to see whether I was listening (of course I was; I knew this was an important moment for her) but to make sure I was ready to handle whatever she had to tell me. I nodded imperceptibly. She continued.

"Myself, and several others, were above the eightieth floor and headed into the stairwell. At every floor below us, crowds of people exited onto the stairs, slowing all of us down. It seemed like forever before we got outside. It was pure chaos. We were eventually herded onto a ferry and taken to New Jersey…at least those of us who made it out. Those who stayed behind all died."

The waitress appeared with our salads and a fresh refill of my coffee. Lainey dug into her food and switched the topic to the play we had just seen. No more of her 9/11 experience. As always we analyzed the various elements of the theatrical production, never alluding to the content. Then our conversation turned to light-hearted issues. I guess the discussion of that traumatic day was done. As we left the restaurant, Lainey suggested a walk along the Hudson River to our respective apartments downtown.

It was one of those early summer evenings. A waning sun glistened off the now calm, almost smooth surface of the river, fresh breezes suggested that all was well. Life could do no wrong. When we were halfway home, Lainey stopped, walked over to a railing, and watched as the water began to roil a bit, her breathing now labored. She pointed across the river.

"That's where they took us on the ferry. Hundreds of us had made it out. They assured us we were now safe."

I looked toward New Jersey as I watched my friend reliving the event from the corner of my eye.

"The first day back at work at our new location, those of us who had survived threw ourselves into each other's arms, crying and hugging, seeing for the first time who had made it out and who hadn't. We told our bosses that we needed counseling to do our jobs, and they got it for us. But it took a long time before we could really concentrate—not just on work, on anything."

Later, as I was writing this section of *The Rule Breakers*, I asked Lainey if I could share these details.

"It's fine," she said. "Enough time has passed."

But is that really true? Not just for Lainey or the others who escaped the towers while their coworkers perished inside, or those of us in Manhattan that day, or the rest of our country? Although the scars remain, the resilience of the American people, their ability to bounce back and not only resume life but to come out of it better and stronger than before, is a testament to who we are as a nation.

I'm so proud of all of us, but on a personal level, I'm especially proud of my lifelong friend, Lainey.

FINAL THOUGHTS

At my fiftieth birthday party, a friend asked me how I would know whether my life had been successful. Sounds like a conversational ploy to celebrate a milestone in one's life. But a few weeks later, I actually sat down and thought about the question.

I knew a successful life did not mean amassing great wealth or attaining international fame. How many individuals who had neatly checked off those boxes had seen their life implode? There seemed to be an endless stream of addictions, suicides, broken marriages, estrangements from children, criminal charges that involved the rich and famous. No, neither of those external symbols assured a successful life. True, it's nice to have enough money and no financial stress; being famous might be fun for a while, everyone wanting to be your friend, photographs taken endlessly. But how do you know who's being real in your life, and who's just playing you for what they can get?

Once you step into the spotlight, on any forum, you become idealized by those who cannot empower themselves and who ascribe traits to you that you may or may not have. Then, too, you can find yourself subjected to the reverse: the haters and bullies, who also don't know you. Remember what my mother told me as a child: *The only people who hurt others are those who are hurt themselves.* There's constructive criticism and then there is acting out to fulfill one's own need to feel better about oneself. Again it comes down to self-empowerment.

Those who know how to validate themselves don't need other people, especially strangers, to do the deed for them.

As I sat wondering whether my life was a success, I realized for myself I had only one criteria to judge success by: when I lay dying, how many people standing around my bedside would have a genuine hole in their heart once I was no longer there? Although that space would eventually heal over, I hoped a small part of it would remain empty, missing me.

*

One day in early spring, I was sitting in the backyard of my home with Coni reading a book. I still missed my Brooklyn stoop, but it was nice to have nature so available. I had to laugh. When we first moved into the home, I had looked out the window and had a fright.

"Coni! Coni!" I yelled. "Come quickly."

"What is it?" she yelled from the bedroom. She came running into the living room.

"Look, look," I said. "There's a wild boar in the driveway!"

Coni looked outside then burst into hysterics. When she recovered, she placed her arm around me, "That's called a possum," she said with a tolerant smile on her face.

"How the hell would I know what a possum looks like?" I replied. "I'm from Brooklyn."

As I sat there on that early spring day, inhaling the lovely aroma of recently blossomed lilacs, I saw movement to my right. I looked over: a squirrel sat right next to me. A chipmunk couple scurried near his feet until they disappeared into a secret hideaway.

To my left, a little farther on, a rabbit with a white fluff ball of a tail sat snacking on a treat it had gathered. And farther over was our groundhog, who'd we'd named Wendy, and who wintered under our shed.

I heard all manner of birds singing and calling to each other: cardinals, sparrows, red-winged blackbirds, redheaded woodpeckers, doves, grackles, titmice, and chickadees.

All species, a few feet from each other. Sometimes a few inches. All of us basking in a spring afternoon, all comfortably going about our business, trusting we would not be harmed by the others, enjoying the day together in peace and harmony.

I thought back on all of the hundreds of people I had worked with over the years: all cultures, all religions, different economic levels, different educational levels. And I wondered how a small, Jewish girl growing up on the streets of Brooklyn could have gained the trust of so many?

Somehow, I was able to dig down past the externals to speak the universal language of the unspoken. The language we speak to our baby infants, our pets—and to the different species in our backyards and parks.

It is a language that says, "I see you. You're okay. You can trust me."

I'm still amazed at how many others not only let me help them, but shared their innermost thoughts, feelings, vulnerabilities, confessed their perceived sins, their hopes, and, most of all, shared their souls with me.

To all of you, I just want to say, thank you.

ACKNOWLEDGMENTS

I'd like to thank my first three readers, Marie Streno, Rosemary Goldford, Bianca Cody Murphy, whose suggestions and support pushed me forward in each of my early drafts of the manuscript, and author Robert Lovinger who gave me a crash course in self-publishing.

A special thank you to Elizabeth Kracht, my developmental editor, for her insightful suggestions, and to the staff at BookBaby, especially Christina Ellis, for sharing their skills while guiding me through the publishing process.

In addition to my early readers, a warm hug to the rest of my circle of friends, Arlene Blecher, Sue Buerkel, Joan Graham, Denise Hernaiz, Judy Hollander, Bonnie Marty, Lee Zevy.

And most of all Toni, for loving me and urging me onward every time I turned my back on this project.

To all of the above, I am very grateful.

ABOUT THE AUTHOR

Peri B. Mann (pseudonym) is a retired licensed clinical social worker in the state of New York, where she currently resides.

She has worked inside an all-male psychiatric prison, on an all-male thirty-day detox unit in a hospital, spent several years as a probation officer, and was the assistant head of the counseling department in an outpatient methadone clinic.

She is a member of the National Association of Social Workers, the Academy of Certified Social Workers, and the Phi Beta Kappa Society.